NEW DIRECTIONS FOR HIGHER EDUCATION

Martin Kramer, *University of California, Berkeley*
EDITOR-IN-CHIEF

Administrative Careers and the Marketplace

Kathryn M. Moore
Michigan State University

Susan B. Twombly
University of Kansas

EDITORS

Number 72, Winter 1990

JOSSEY-BASS INC., PUBLISHERS
San Francisco

ADMINISTRATIVE CAREERS AND THE MARKETPLACE
Kathryn M. Moore, Susan B. Twombly (eds.)
New Directions for Higher Education, no. 72
Volume XVIII, number 4
Martin Kramer, Editor-in-Chief

Microfilm copies of issues and articles are available in 16mm and 35mm,
as well as microfiche in 105mm, through University Microfilms Inc., 300
North Zeeb Road, Ann Arbor, Michigan 48106.

LC 85-644752   ISSN 0271-0560   ISBN 1-55542-808-8

NEW DIRECTIONS FOR HIGHER EDUCATION is part of The Jossey-Bass
Higher and Adult Education Series and is published quarterly by Jossey-
Bass Inc., Publishers (publication number USPS 990-880). Second-class
postage paid at San Francisco, California, and at additional mailing
offices. Postmaster: Send address changes to Jossey-Bass Inc., Publishers,
350 Sansome Street, San Francisco, California 94104.

EDITORIAL CORRESPONDENCE should be sent to the Editor-in-Chief,
Martin Kramer, 2807 Shasta Road, Berkeley, California 94708.

Cover photograph and random dot by Richard Blair/Color & Light
© 1990.

Printed on acid-free paper in the United States of America.

CONTENTS

EDITORS' NOTES

Today, many newcomers are working in colleges and universities as administrators, managers, and nonteaching professionals. Some have come from the faculty, others have not. Each year many eager young people enter master's degree programs in student personnel administration en route to entry-level positions in a variety of administrative support areas. Still others have backgrounds as varied as the individuals themselves. Regardless of background, most want to understand better how to survive and thrive in today's institutions. Most want to build long and productive careers in college and university administration. This volume, *Administrative Careers and the Marketplace*, is intended to introduce newcomers to the way administrative careers work as part of an intricate administrative marketplace in higher education.

Colleges and universities have changed considerably since one individual, the president, performed all administrative functions. They have become complex organizations with many administrative positions, carrying out a wide variety of tasks directly related to teaching and scholarship as well as functions such as fund-raising, financial management, grants management, and student affairs. For those who begin faculty careers, the route from assistant to full professor is well marked and the criteria for advancement clearly stated in terms appropriate to the mission of each type of postsecondary institution. In contrast, individuals who launch administrative careers are entering relatively uncharted waters. Although sociologists and management scholars have long recognized the importance of careers to individuals, to organizations, and to society and have devoted much attention to understanding the nature of career mobility in many types of organizations, relatively little attention has been paid to the careers and career mobility of college and university administrators.

In large measure this lack of attention is a throw-back to several outdated notions. One is that only faculty members can and do fill these important positions, if only on a temporary basis. A second is that no one should aspire (publicly, at least) to or intentionally plan for a career leading to a presidency or other top position. Another common belief is that the presidency is the only important career in college and university administration. It is not surprising, then, that most scholarly interest has focused on career paths of presidents. However, there are dozens of other very important administrative positions that occupy the lives of thousands of competent individuals. Many are filled by people who do not seek a presidency, but who still believe that a career in administration is worth having.

Verla Ensign, at Michigan State University, East Lansing, contributed to the initial preparation of this volume.

1

Although information exists to guide those who aspire to the presidency and a few other positions such as chief student affairs officer, this guidance is available because their professional organizations have devoted considerable attention to career issues. Much of the general career information that is available often is based on personal anecdotes and does not take into consideration the larger marketplace in which administrative careers are developed. Whether they plan to spend two years, ten years, or a lifetime, there is little to guide people at the beginning or midpoint of their careers. But there are many important and useful factors for newcomers as well as veterans to think about as they anticipate career opportunities in the more than three thousand colleges and universities in this country.

In this volume we have accumulated knowledge and experience from many vantage points in order to provide information and insights about administrative careers and the marketplace in postsecondary education. The volume provides important information for moving in the marketplace, including how to decipher hiring practices, how to work with the search process, how to match expectations to the realities of a new position, and how to obtain and use mentors and other career enhancers. All of the authors have addressed their chapters specifically to individuals considering or in the midst of administrative careers.

In Chapter One Susan B. Twombly provides a framework that views careers in administration as systems analogous to highway systems. Career systems facilitate the flow of individuals into, through, and out of organizations. Research on administrators' careers accumulated during the last decade is used to examine three important components of career systems: entry, development (career ladders), and exit. She also considers the unique nature of career systems in colleges and universities and describes multiple career systems shaped by job family or functional area, institutional type, and geographical region.

The majority of administrators (60 percent) make all or part of their careers within a single college or university. In Chapter Two Mary Ann D. Sagaria and Cynthia S. Dickens use recent research to construct five propositions for "thriving at home." They address the issues and concerns of people who choose to make their careers within one institution. They advise insider administrators to take advantage of personnel policies intended to enhance careers of those already employed and to learn how to work within their respective institution's culture in order to be successful. Sagaria and Dickens specifically address policies that affect mobility within a single institution.

Clearly, local knowledge and networks can assist individuals in interpreting position announcements. But how do job-seeking administrators assess hiring practices of the hundreds of colleges and universities whose advertisements appear regularly in the *Chronicle of Higher Education?* In

Chapter Three Michael R. Dingerson suggests that there are many things individuals can learn from job announcements. Further, he provides advice on how to "check out" a search without damaging one's candidacy.

Search committees are an integral component of administrator selection in colleges and universities. As search committees become more sophisticated in their techniques, candidates must become equally adept at working with such committees to get the information they seek and to create favorable impressions of themselves. In a recent study of dean searches, members of search committees expressed surprise at just how unskilled many applicants were at presenting themselves well on paper or in campus interviews. Jane Fiori Lawrence and Theodore J. Marchese, in Chapter Four, provide detailed advice on how to decide what jobs to apply for, how to present oneself in contacts with search committees, and how to prepare for an interview.

Few institutions do an adequate job of career review, career enhancement, or professional development with their administrators. Most administrators must accomplish these tasks for themselves, but there are important issues to consider and numerous choices to be made in crafting a solid set of experiences for oneself. In Chapter Five Sharon A. McDade outlines some of the professional development opportunities that are available and suggests strategies for people to consider in preparing themselves to be better administrators and to have more successful careers.

Mentors can be of great assistance to career advancement for administrators in higher education. Although sponsors can help individuals gain specific positions, mentors engage protégés in long-term personal and professional relationships that involve education and training. In Chapter Six Linda K. Johnsrud uses vignettes to describe both mentor-protégé relationships that are helpful and those that are detrimental to professional development. She suggests several strategies for ensuring effective mentor-protégé relationships.

In Chapter Seven Marlene Ross and Madeleine F. Green use information gathered from the American Council on Education Fellows Program, from research on presidents, and from years of anecdotal data to expose the frequently unwritten, sometimes unspoken, codes, rules, and practices that guide career advancement of deans and other academic administrators. They speak frankly about institutional realities, factors affecting career mobility, and other "rules of the game" for building successful careers. The authors' remarks are applicable to many types of administrators.

One of the realities noted by Ross and Green is that "the title you see is not always what you get." This gap between expectations for a new job and the realities of the position is addressed by Marilyn J. Amey in Chapter Eight. Amey describes elements that contribute to this gap, such as role conflict, scope of responsibilities, lack of feedback, weak or inappropriate academic and experiential preparation, and lack of performance evaluation. Strategies for closing this gap include understanding organizational culture, effective use of confidants and other organizational communication networks, professional anchoring, and career mapping.

Many more women and minority administrators will be working in higher education in the next decades. They still must face and learn to deal with institutions that have not been used to their presence, much less their leadership. In Chapter Nine Kathryn M. Moore discusses ways in which difficult situations generated by the token status of many women and minority administrators today can be turned to the advantage of the individuals and their institutions. Such difficult circumstances include high visibility, isolation, greater professional risk, and a different cultural heritage of care and community.

In Chapter Ten Joseph F. Kauffman, long a keen observer and adviser to presidents and other administrators, discusses the increasing professionalization of administration and the changing conditions in which today's administrators function. He reminds us that aspiring administrators must be committed not only to effective management but also to the central purposes of our colleges and universities: teaching and scholarship. Effective functioning of institutions aimed at achieving their central purpose is the primary goal of administration.

In our concluding comments in Chapter Eleven we point out that collegiate administration is really part of a much larger endeavor, namely, the work of knowledge generation and transmission. A global information society is already forming around a core of institutions that includes but is not limited to colleges and universities. Administrators can benefit by seeing their work in this larger context. If they do, they will see the need for building a personal agenda of lifelong learning. They also will see their work in one college as a way to prepare themselves for a larger marketplace and a more varied career in the future. This larger vista is worth pondering both on a personal level and for the benefit of the colleges and universities where administrators serve.

Kathryn M. Moore
Susan B. Twombly
Editors

Kathryn M. Moore is professor of educational policy and leadership in the Department of Educational Administration at Michigan State University, East Lansing.

Susan B. Twombly is assistant professor of higher education in the Department of Educational Policy and Administration at the University of Kansas, Lawrence.

Administrative careers are characterized by ill-defined career paths, multiple entrance points, and lack of explicit criteria for determining mobility.

Career Maps and Institutional Highways

Susan B. Twombly

During the past several decades administrative employment opportunities in higher education have increased dramatically (Grassmuck, 1990). Growth, particularly of administrative support areas such as grants administration, alumni affairs, development, and student affairs, provides increasing opportunities not only for jobs but also for individuals to develop careers as college and university administrators. However, numerous and diverse opportunities only serve to increase rather than decrease confusion surrounding administrative careers in higher education. As Kathryn M. Moore (1984, p. 2) stated in her presidential address to the Association for the Study of Higher Education, "The people who launch themselves into careers in administration often do not know how to maneuver. They sometimes do not know where they want to go. They may not even realize they are part of a large, interconnected network."

A college or university administrative career can be defined as a "series of jobs involving tasks of governance and management that over time tend to have increasing responsibility, reward, and recognition" (Moore, 1984, p. 160). Highway systems are apt metaphors for administrative careers in higher education. Careers have entry and exit points and multiple paths between destinations. Travel along administrative career paths is guided by direction signs, speed limits, and other "rules" to assure orderly travel. However, in contrast to some organizations, the highways and byways of administrative careers in higher education are not well marked; the road signs are often subtle. As Moore (1984, p. 3) noted, "The entry and exit signs are not nearly as well marked as they are on freeways. And there are precious few roadcrews working to keep the usual routes in good repair. You feel you could use a good map. But there are none." The purpose of this chapter is to provide such a map of the major landmarks of administrative careers, based on research of the past decade. There is a danger in this approach: By identifying the routes, entry points, and other dimensions of careers as they have existed in the past, we run the risk of reinforcing traditional routes that have not been equally accessible to all groups of individuals. Furthermore, much of the research on careers in the last forty years, including my own, assumes traditional conceptions of twentieth-century bureaucracies. Feminists and other critics argue that this view of careers is rooted in patriarchy and is not an accurate reflection of careers as experienced by women. For these reasons it is not my intention to offer prescriptions about administrative careers based on past research. The aim, rather, is to provide a larger framework for organizational careers within which individuals can consider their own career options and possibilities.

Career Systems

Like cities, states, and nations that have highway systems to direct the flow of traffic, colleges and universities have career systems to guide the flow of individuals through administrative positions. These systems consist of "the collection of policies, priorities, and actions that organizations use to manage the flow of their members into, through, and out of the organizations over time" (Sonnenfeld and Peiperl, 1988, p. 588). In other words, career systems consist of the various formal and informal factors that recruit individuals and direct their movement along various career paths. Career systems consist of three main elements: entry, development (for example, career ladders, training), and exit.

Before these components of career systems are discussed, we must examine distinctive characteristics of colleges and universities that affect the nature and number of institutional highways over which career mobility occurs. There are several important factors that affect the length and shape of the routes and the speed at which individuals can move in order to develop careers in postsecondary education. First, career systems reflect the structure of the organizations they serve. Colleges and universities have relatively flat hierarchies with few top-level and many midlevel positions. Consequently, there is more room for career mobility within the ranks of middle management, and opportunities for upward mobility to the few top-level positions are restricted. As a result career mobility is often accomplished in other ways such as adding responsibilities to existing positions, which sometimes leads to the creation of new positions (Miner and Estler, 1985), changing position titles to reflect excellent work, and increasing lateral mobility to positions that have the same title but more responsibility at larger institutions (Scott, 1978; Twombly, 1988).

A second important characteristic of colleges and universities is that they have multiple administrative hierarchies. There are an academic administrative hierarchy overseeing the core work of the college or university (that is, teaching, research, and service) and multiple administrative hierarchies responsible for activities that support these core functions. Past experience and research suggest that these hierarchies have relatively separate career systems. College and university presidents are more likely to be products of academic career systems than of one or another of the administrative support career systems. However, as discussed later in this chapter, in reality presidents, like other professionals, have diverse career experiences.

Entry. The first component of career systems in postsecondary education is entry. Entry is approached from two perspectives: institutional and individual.

Institutional Perspective. From the college or university's point of view, entry involves planning for human resource needs and recruiting and selecting individuals to fill positions—building the highways, providing entrance points, and posting signs. Responsibility for human resource planning for administrative personnel typically rests at the department or division level rather than in a centralized office and often occurs sporadically and rather haphazardly. Hiring policies and procedures, as Dingerson demonstrates in Chapter Three, may differ greatly from one unit to another, although affirmative action guidelines may have standardized at least some aspects of the job recruitment process. Often overlooked, institutional and unit policies regarding recruitment and staff selection can have substantial impact on career mobility. Sagaria and Dickens discuss this further in Chapter Two.

In addition, recruitment and selection for administrative positions are typically performed by search committees consisting of representatives of the hiring unit. Colleges and universities obtain candidates for administrative vacancies by directly advertising through media such as the *Chronicle of Higher Education.* Few institutions or state college and university systems develop and maintain vitae banks for administrative positions. Furthermore, although encouraged to recruit aggressively through personal contacts, colleges and universities are frequently passive in their recruitment efforts, placing advertisements and waiting for candidates to apply. Individuals seeking entry or midlevel positions may actively seek positions, but administrators already in top-level positions are typically not actively seeking positions, thus reinforcing the need for aggressive recruitment efforts. The notable exception to advertising-as-recruitment occurs in presidential searches, which increasingly rely on consulting firms to generate and screen candidates. Although the hiring unit may have written policies governing whether positions must be advertised nationally, regionally, or only within an institution, search committees are often left to determine how aggressively a search for candidates is conducted. Affirmative action guidelines, depending on how they are enacted by an institution, can influence this aspect of administrator recruitment.

Where does the supply of individuals come from to fill administrative positions? There are two dimensions to the issue of supply. One dimension is whether individuals come from positions within higher education or from positions outside of higher education. Dingerson (Chapter Three) presents a somewhat different slant on this dimension by asking whether individuals come from traditional versus nontraditional sources. The other dimension is whether individuals move within one institution or among colleges and universities. Some administrative positions and some types of colleges are more open than others to recruiting individuals directly from jobs outside of higher education. For example, academic deanships may not be as open to external markets as other positions such as chief business officer. Community colleges in general appear to be more open to hiring individuals from outside of higher education than are four-year colleges and universities.

Administrative careers develop within a labor market that is not necessarily bound by a single college. Indeed, they frequently span several institutions. Colleges and universities may prefer to make internal appointments, particularly for midlevel positions, as opposed to advertising and hiring regionally or nationally. An individual may build a career within the area of student affairs, for example, by holding jobs in several different institutions. This is particularly true of careers of presidents and other top-level administrators (Kerr and Gade, 1986). However, despite the old adage that "one must move out in order to move up," a substantial and growing number of administrators build their careers within one college or university (Sagaria and Johnsrud, 1987). The parallel choices of colleges and universities to hire from within or from other institutions and of individuals to stay within one institution or to move interinstitutionally have many ramifications for career mobility. Individuals who choose to build careers within one institution may have to think differently and creatively about options and goals. Sagaria and Dickens discuss the dynamics of building a career within a single institution in Chapter Two.

Individual Perspective. From an individual's point of view, entry refers to finding out about administrative vacancies, making the decision to change jobs, and becoming a candidate for a position. This activity occurs in a marketplace and is guided by a matching process in which employers, positions, and eligible candidates are brought together.

What motivates individuals to seek careers in administration and to enter the job market? Tradition would have us believe that individuals who enter academic administration (academic dean, provost, and so on) do so by default, as a natural progression of participation in faculty governance or other service roles, or because they are unsuccessful as faculty members. The assumption guiding these unfounded stories is that administration is not a "real" career; administration is merely a temporary side-trip from the main (faculty) road. However, for both two-year and four-year college and university administrators, personal challenge and the duties and responsibilities of a new job were rated as the primary factors motivating individuals to seek their current positions (Moore, 1983; Moore, Twombly, and Martorana, 1985; Kerr and Gade, 1986). "Ready for a change" was another important factor pushing individuals to seek their current administrative positions. Geographical location and congeniality of colleagues are also frequently mentioned as factors pulling administrators to their current positions.

With respect to the matching process from the individual's point of view, the job market seems to function fairly straightforwardly and formally. In a national study of two-year college administrators, most administrators reported learning about current positions through formal job announcements from the hiring institution, and most reported making formal application (Twombly and Moore, 1987). Personal contacts, which are thought to provide more trustworthy information than formal job announcements, were also important both as sources of information about jobs and as catalysts in nominating individuals for positions. As such, it was somewhat surprising that mentors, influential in other aspects of administrative career mobility, were not as helpful in providing job opening information as were more generalized personal contacts (Twombly and Moore, 1987). These findings suggest that networks of general personal contacts can be helpful to individuals seeking administrative positions in higher education.

The search process and search committees are key players in the matching process in higher education. In Chapter Four, Lawrence and Marchese provide useful advice for individuals on how to confront the search committee and the recruitment process in general, so the search process is not discussed here.

Development: The Structure of Administrative Careers. The developmental aspect of career systems involves socialization, training, career planning, succession planning, and promotions (Sonnenfeld and Peiperl, 1988). In modern organizations career ladders, paths, or lines are considered the means by which the functions of socialization, training, and promotion are accomplished (Becker and Strauss, 1966; Doeringer and Piore, 1971). The ideal career ladder from this perspective is one in which positions are clearly identified and tightly ordered in a sequence of increasing responsibility and reward. Learning that occurs in a lower-level position on the ladder prepares individuals to assume the next higher position in a sequence. This model implies that individuals enter careers through designated entry points and only compete with others who also entered at the same respective points for promotion to higher-level positions. The structure is analogous to that of a highly organized tour in which each stopping point is clearly identified and information gained by tourists in one stop is necessary for the next stop on the route. Tour participants do not have to compete with other tourists for rides, food, and shelter. These items are all taken care of by the tour organizers once each individual gains entry to the tour. Career theorists have argued that this is an efficient way for organizations to socialize, train, and obtain commitment from employees. However, this ideal-type career is only a partially accurate description of administrative careers in higher education.

Despite many myths, administrative career paths in both two-year and four-year colleges are relatively unstructured. There are multiple pathways to nearly every top-level position, including the presidency. A rather pervasive myth suggests that the route to the presidency of four-year colleges and universities follows a straight path beginning with a faculty entry point and proceeding through the positions of department chair, dean, provost, and then president (Cohen and March, 1976). However, a study based on a national sample of presidents found that fifteen different variations on this hypothesized career path were necessary to capture all of the presidents' careers (Moore, Salimbene, Marlier, and Bragg, 1983). Only 3 percent of 156 presidents actually followed the normative career trajectory. The single most common path for presidents was from faculty member to an administrative position other than dean or provost and then to president, but this route was taken by only 16 percent of the presidents. A faculty position is overwhelmingly the entry point for presidents of four-year colleges and universities; however, 95 percent of all presidents have administrative experience in higher education (Kerr and Gade, 1986). The main route to the presidency in two-year colleges is through a chief academic officer position, but other top-level administrative positions are much less likely to serve as stepping-stones to presidencies (Twombly, 1988). In fact, increasingly, the best way to become a two-year college president is to already be one. Vaughan (1986) describes a scenario in which new, two-year college presidents begin looking for another presidency the minute they step on campus. Two-year college presidents are also most likely to begin their careers as faculty members, but dean or director administrative positions also served as entry points for a substantial number of presidents. Despite the wide variation in actual paths to the presidency, belief in Cohen and March's (1976) normative career path is so strong as to potentially influence both the gatekeepers who hire and potential applicants who, in believing the myth, are hesitant to apply if they have nontraditional career histories.

A shortened version of the normative presidential career trajectory is an equally unsatisfactory representation of academic deans' careers in four-year colleges and universities. However, there are fewer variations of the path to an academic deanship. A faculty position is also the typical entry point for deans. However, relatively few individuals move from faculty to department chair, to assistant or associate dean, to dean (Moore, Salimbene, Marlier, and Bragg, 1983). Arts or graduate deans tend to follow a traditional path from faculty, to department chair, to dean, but professional school deans often skip intermediate positions and jump directly from faculty positions to deanships. Deans who do not have faculty experience are most likely found in divisions such as continuing education. There are a variety of paths to the two-year college chief academic officer position as well. Although the path to the chief academic post frequently includes an assistant or associate position, a "traditional" path leading from faculty, to department head, to dean is relatively untraveled. The entry point for two-year college chief academic officers is typically also a faculty position; however, a surprising number started their careers as administrators (Twombly, 1988).

Somewhat more traditional career paths can be identified for chief business officers and other top-level administrators in support areas in both two-year and four-year colleges and universities. Chief business officers in both sectors who move intra-institutionally move through an assistant or associate business position to the chief business post. Chief business officers are somewhat unusual in that over 20 percent in four-year institutions and 40 percent in two-year institutions assume their positions directly from outside of postsecondary education (Twombly, 1988; Stauffer, 1990). The careers of chief student affairs officers in two-year colleges resemble a traditional career path much more closely than do paths to other top-level positions in this institutional sector. The beginning point of paths to the chief student affairs position typically is an assistant or associate position with stopping points at another assistant or associate position and perhaps a director position.

Another aspect of career development is training. In addition to on-the-job training, there are two other types of training: organization or job-specific training (staff development) and more generalized training that cuts across specific organizations, such as found at the Harvard Institute for Educational Management. Little is known about the types of institutionally based training administrators receive and how such training contributes to career advancement. When asked about important internal professional development activities, two-year college administrators noted the importance of opportunities to take on additional responsibilities and of formal written performance review to career advancement. Temporary task or job rotation and career review were important but not widely available internal forms of training (Moore, Twombly, and Martorana, 1985). When asked about external activities that contributed to career advancement, four-year college and university administrators reported consulting, publishing, and holding a seat on a state or regional professional association board of directors (Moore, 1983). Two-year college administrators also reported consulting and membership on state or regional boards as important to career advancement (Moore, Twombly, and Martorana, 1985). Moreover, as discussed later, it may well be that some of the most influential and important "training" is done by mentors.

It is surprising that relatively few two-year or four-year administrators indicated that they had participated in formal training opportunities such as provided by the Harvard Institute for Educational Management, Bryn Mawr, and the American Council on Education (ACE) Fellows Program (Moore, 1983). In two-year colleges, the National Institute for Leadership Development and Leadership 2000 are two formal training programs that seem to be growing in popularity. The National Institute for Leadership Development specifically serves women in community colleges and reports a high correlation between participation and career mobility (Desjardins, personal communication, 1990). Programs such as the ACE fellowships report similar success for those who participate (Chibucos and Green, 1989). McDade (Chapter Five) identifies the positive impact of formal administrator development programs.

Exit. Career research typically is focused on people who hold positions at the time of each study. Consequently, we know little about why individuals leave careers in higher education before retirement age. The little we do know about those who step down from presidencies is anecdotal in nature and is often information obtained from their successors. Kerr and Gade (1986) observed that a president typically serves seven years in one presidency and then moves on to another presidency, back to the faculty, to other administrative positions, to retirement or semiretirement, or to jobs outside of higher education. Options open to retiring administrators are shaped by age at which exit occurs and the reasons for stepping down from administration.

Assigning People to Positions: Determinants of Career Mobility. Determinants of career mobility include not only the criteria by which personnel selections are made but also the pace at which individuals develop their careers. Job change rather than promotion is the predominant means by which administrators in higher education obtain new jobs of increasing responsibility, reward, and recognition. The rate at which individuals change jobs is determined by a number of factors, among them the vacancy rate, the growth rate, and demographics. The vacancy rate is a particularly important determinant of advancement opportunities for individuals in higher education. Relatively flat hierarchies dictate that there are fewer and fewer outlets as one moves to higher levels of the administrative ranks; as a result, individuals moving internally may have to wait for years for a single chief student affairs position to become available and then have to compete for the position with other applicants. During the past decade, however, turnover and growth in the number of positions has allowed for relatively fast-paced mobility. A majority of four-year college and university administrators surveyed in 1981 and two-year college administrators surveyed in 1984 had been in their current positions five years or less. The changing age structure of U.S. society suggests that the pace on administrative career highways will remain fast.

Although the criteria by which any single selection decision is made are unique to the position and to the hiring unit, it is possible to identify general factors that influence career mobility in colleges and universities. Some of these factors are touched on only briefly here as other authors in this volume discuss them more fully.

Education. Nearly all individuals holding presidencies, provostships, and academic deanships in both two-year and four-year colleges and universities have doctoral degrees (Moore, 1983; Moore, Twombly, and Martorana, 1985; Kerr and Gade, 1986). Other top-line administrators such as chief student affairs officers or chief business officers are less likely to hold doctoral degrees; however, the prevalence of the doctorate among chief student affairs officers is growing. Research on two-year college administrators' careers suggests that many earn their doctorates after they begin their careers. This is not surprising since the master's degree is the preferred credential for teaching in community colleges and for entry-level administrative posts in all types of institutions. The student composition of doctoral programs in higher education and in student personnel administration confirms this pattern of doctoral study for many aspiring administrators.

The preferred type of doctorate varies by type of institution and position. Presidents, provosts, and academic deans in four-year colleges and universities overwhelmingly hold doctorates in academic disciplines such as history and chemistry (Moore, 1983; Ross and Green, this volume). A majority of presidents of community colleges hold doctorates in the fields of higher education, student personnel administration, or educational administration. In a recent study Townsend and Weise (in press) found that the higher education degree was preferred over a doctorate in a traditional academic discipline for chief student affairs, chief business officer, and other institutional management positions by over 50 percent of community college respondents and 42 percent of the four-year college and university respondents. Conversely, a higher education doctorate was less preferred to a doctorate in a discipline for presidencies and other academic administrative positions. But the community college presidency was an exception to this preference for doctorates in traditional disciplines.

Age. Seniority per se is not a criterion for advancement in administrative careers. That is, seniority is not the primary determinant of career mobility, although presidents and other top-line administrators have "paid their dues" in the system. In fact, Sagaria and Moore (1983) found a preference for youth, that is, a declining mobility with increasing age in selections for college and university administrative positions. Some mobility opportunities for older administrators are maintained, however. Presidents and provosts tend to be somewhat older than individuals holding other top-line positions. The largest percentage of presidents and provosts of both two-year and four-year institutions is found in the age group forty-five to fifty-five, a trend that has remained fairly consistent over the years. Because of the youth preference that seems to operate in higher education, age of presidents has implications for the mobility opportunities of provosts and other chief academic officers (or other administrators) who aspire to presidencies. It would appear that the older an individual becomes, the lower the chances of moving upward to a presidency (Moore, 1983; Moore, Twombly, and Martorana, 1985). These studies have also revealed age discrepancies by sex. Women were equally represented in younger but not older cohorts. These findings suggest differential career effects of age between women and men. Ten years ago, the forty- to fifty-year-old women who competed for top positions were relatively rare. These women were exceptional and drew much attention. Now the younger groups, which are much more gender balanced, are at the age when men are competing with more women and women are competing with each other for the same top-level positions. Women may actually have a slight edge when competing for positions in underutilized administrative units identified by affirmative action guidelines.

Gender. Women accounted for less than one-quarter of all administrators in a national study of four-year college and university administrators completed in 1981 and a comparable study of two-year college administrators completed in 1984 (Moore, 1983; Moore, Twombly, and Martorana, 1985). Furthermore, women were proportionally overrepresented in certain types of positions, namely, head librarians and directors of financial aid (Moore, 1983). In two-year colleges, the top three positions for women were head librarian, director of financial aid, and chief academic officer; director of continuing education was a close fourth. In contrast, the positions of president, chief business officer, and registrar were predominantly held by men (Moore, Twombly, and Martorana, 1985). One could expect this situation to have changed substantially in the ten years since the first study was completed; however, indications are that it has not. Vaughan (1989) reports that 8 percent of community college presidencies are held by women. This figure is no higher than the percentage in 1984 (Moore, Twombly, and Martorana, 1985).

Race and Ethnicity. The situation for minorities is even more dismal than for women. In 1981, only 5 percent of a national sample of four-year college and university administrators were black, and all other racial and ethnic groups together comprised only 3 percent of the sample (Moore, 1983). The composition of the two-year college administrative ranks did not look much different in 1984. Only 5 percent were black, while 4 percent were other minority groups. Vaughan (1989) reports that 4 percent of community college presidents are black and only 2 percent are Hispanic. Although there has been no recent national census of the percentage of women and minorities holding administrative positions in higher education, we can safely conclude that women and minorities are not represented among administrative positions at the same rate as they are among students. Women do have a better chance of advancing in some areas of specialization than in others.

There are at least three plausible explanations for the fact that women and minorities are so vastly underrepresented in top-level administrative positions in higher education. One is that women and minorities have not had the requisite experiences to qualify for such positions. A second is that women and minorities have not aspired to top-level posts. A third is that a glass ceiling exists for women and minorities, curtailing their mobility opportunities. As more and more women and minorities have gained the necessary professional degrees and experiences and have aspired to such positions during the last decade, we are left with the challenge of understanding how and why gender, race, and ethnicity still seem to preclude access to top-level positions. Moore (Chapter Nine) discusses the challenges of achieving and benefiting from diversity.

Mentors. The role and importance of mentors to the career advancement of administrators in higher education is well documented (for example, Simeone, 1984; Moore, 1988). Over half of all two-year and four-year administrators reported that they had had mentors who had been helpful, particularly in the early stages of their careers (Moore, 1983; Moore, Twombly, and Martorana, 1985). Presidents were particularly likely to have benefited from mentors. Administrators who have benefited from mentors are also more likely to serve as mentors of others (Moore, Twombly, and Martorana, 1985). General guidance and role modeling seem to be the most important function of mentors. Johnsrud (Chapter Six) discusses the nature of the mentoring relationship in more detail, providing guidance on how these relationships can be helpful and how to avoid harmful mentor relationships.

Multiple Career Systems

As stated at the outset of this chapter, colleges and universities are characterized by multiple career systems. These systems occur at a variety of levels: by functional area or job family, by institutional type, and by geographical region. It should be noted that institutional prestige and type of control (public or private) also are thought to affect career mobility, but these two factors are not discussed in this chapter. Each career system has its own entrance, development, and exit patterns, and there may or may not be interconnecting links between these career systems.

Job Family or Functional Area. In addition to the distinction between academic administrative career systems and administrative support-area career systems, there are multiple career systems shaped by job family or functional area. As administrative specialties mature, the practitioners seek individuals from among their own ranks to fill administrative posts. This is particularly true for top-level posts. Cross-area mobility that does occur is typically between low-level rather than top-level positions (Twombly, 1988). Furthermore, within the general area of administrative services and student affairs, for example, there are multiple career systems such as student organizations and activities, counseling, and housing. Each may constitute its own career system. Generally speaking it is very difficult to cross over from an administrative support area to academic administration (dean, provost) without faculty experience, while the reverse does not happen often but does occur. The academic career system has been the major supplier of presidents. This is an unfortunate situation, not because academic administrators do not make good presidents but because there are many highly creative and competent individuals in administrative support areas. Also, administrative support areas are more likely to be sources of female and minority presidential candidates.

Institution Type. Institution type can provide a powerful boundary between career systems (Smolansky, 1984). Research universities, liberal arts colleges, community colleges, and public and private institutions seem to have relatively self-contained career systems. When interinstitutional mobility occurs, it is usually among institutions of the same type. Whether institution type constitutes a barrier to career mobility because individuals prefer to stay within a single type of institution or because they are not selected when they do apply for positions in a different type of institution is not known. In the absence of highly structured career ladders, hiring from institutions similar in mission and complexity reduces the disruption associated with changes in personnel. When individuals do cross over from one type of college or university to another, some sort of exchange is likely to be involved: a higher-level position in a smaller or lower-prestige institution to a lower-level position in a larger or higher-prestige institution. It is widely recognized that it is easier to move down in the prestige hierarchy of institutions than it is to move up. However, it is no longer the case that individuals can readily move from positions in four-year institutions to positions in community colleges, which at one time drew substantially from four-year colleges and universities (Twombly, 1987).

Geographical Region. Geographical region provides a surprisingly strong boundary between career systems for both two-year and four-year colleges and universities (Smolansky, 1984; Clark, Twombly, and Moore, in press). This is particularly true in community colleges where over half of interinstitutional movement took place on a within-state basis. Even presidents and chief academic officers who appeared to be least affected by state lines still tended to stay within state in sufficient proportions to clearly establish state boundaries as a compelling factor in administrator mobility. Individual preference, regional contacts, and institutional preference for local knowledge are contributing factors to the tendency for administrators to move within a given region. Familiarity with state and regional characteristics is particularly helpful in the community college setting and is increasingly important among publicly controlled state colleges and universities.

Conclusion

The administrative marketplace is characterized by ill-defined career paths, multiple entrance points, and lack of explicit criteria for determining mobility. The advantage of relatively unstructured career systems is that individuals with diverse backgrounds are afforded many opportunities to navigate the sometimes confusing, interconnecting network of positions and institutions that make up the multiple career systems of higher education. The disadvantage is that it is difficult to give sound advice to those seeking administrative careers. "Rules" governing mobility are often part of a particular institution's culture. For example, the fact that recent provosts have been internal appointments translates to "the provost position at this institution is reserved for internal appointments." Positions do have "histories" too, and prospective administrators would do well to be aware of this dimension when considering a specific position. Furthermore, for every rule or pattern identified in administrative careers, an exception can be named.

Despite this seeming confusion, there are identifiable components of administrative career systems in higher education. Knowledge of these various systems and their diverse dimensions can provide some direction to individuals as they begin the important adventure of pursuing administrative careers in higher education.

References

Becker, H., and Strauss, A. "Careers, Personality, and Adult Socialization." *American Journal of Sociology,* 1966, *62,* 253–263.

Chibucos, T., and Green, M. "Leadership Development in Higher Education: An Evaluation of the ACE Fellows Program." *Journal of Higher Education,* 1989, *60* (1), 21–42.

Clark, B., Twombly, S., and Moore, K. "Inter-Institutional Job Mobility in Two-Year Colleges and Institutional Characteristics." *Community/Junior College Quarterly of Research and Practice,* in press.

Cohen, M., and March, J. *Leadership and Ambiguity: The American College President.* New York: McGraw-Hill, 1976.

Doeringer, P., and Piore, M. *Internal Labor Markets and Manpower Analysis.* Lexington, Mass: Heath Lexington, 1971.

Grassmuck, K. "Big Increases in Academic-Support Staffs Prompt Growing Concerns on Campuses." *Chronicle of Higher Education,* Mar. 28, 1990, pp. A1, A32.

Kerr, C., and Gade, M. L. *The Many Lives of Academic Presidents: Time, Place, and*

Character. Washington, D.C.: Association of Governing Boards of Universities and Colleges, 1986.

Miner, A., and Estler, S. "Accrual Mobility: Job Mobility in Higher Education Through Responsibility Accrual." *Journal of Higher Education,* 1985, *56,* 121-143.

Moore, K. M. *Leaders in Transition: A National Study of Higher Education Administrators.* University Park: Center for the Study of Higher Education, The Pennsylvania State University, 1983.

Moore, K. M. "The Structure of Administrative Careers: A Prose Poem in Four Parts." *Review of Higher Education,* 1984, *8* (4), 1-14.

Moore, K. M. "Administrative Careers: Multiple Pathways to Leadership Positions." In M. Green (ed.), *Leaders for a New Era: Strategies for Higher Education.* New York: American Council on Education and Macmillan, 1988.

Moore, K. M., Salimbene, A., Marlier, J., and Bragg, S. "The Structure of Presidents and Deans Careers." *Journal of Higher Education,* 1983, *54* (4), 501-515.

Moore, K. M., Twombly, S. B., and Martorana, S. V. *Today's Academic Leaders: A National Study of Administrators in Two-Year Colleges.* University Park: Center for the Study of Higher Education, The Pennsylvania State University, 1985.

Sagaria, M.A.D., and Johnsrud, L. K. *Many Are Candidates, But Few Compete: The Impact of Internal Promotion Change of Administrators and Professional Staff on White Women and Minorities.* Columbus: Department of Educational Policy and Leadership, Ohio State University, 1987.

Sagaria, M.A.D., and Moore, K. M. "Job Change and Age: The Experience of Administrators in Colleges and Universities." *Sociological Spectrum,* 1983, *3,* 353-370.

Scott, R. *Lords, Squires, and Yoemen: Collegiate Middle-Managers and Their Organizations.* AAHE-ASHE Higher Education Research Report No. 7. Washington, D.C.: American Association for Higher Education, 1978.

Simeone, A. *Academic Women.* Amherst, Mass.: Bergen & Garvey, 1984.

Smolansky, B. "Job-Transition Behavior in the Labor Market for Administrators in Higher Education." Unpublished doctoral dissertation, Department of Sociology, The Pennsylvania State University, 1984.

Sonnenfeld, J., and Peiperl, M. "Staffing Policy as a Strategic Response: A Typology of Career Systems." *Academy of Management Review,* 1988, *13,* 588-600.

Stauffer, G. L. "Career Patterns of Chief Business Officers at Four-Year Institutions of Higher Education." Unpublished doctoral dissertation. Department of Educational Policy and Administration, University of Kansas, 1990.

Townsend, B., and Weise, M. "Value of the Doctorate in Higher Education for Student Affairs Administrators." *NASPA Journal,* in press.

Twombly, S. B. "Administrative Labor Markets: A Test of the Existence of Internal Labor Markets in Two-Year Colleges." *Journal of Higher Education,* 1988, *59* (6), 668-689.

Twombly, S. B., and Moore, K. M. "Career Change Among Community College Administrators." *Review of Higher Education,* 1987, *11* (1), 17-38.

Vaughan, G. B. *The Community College Presidency.* New York: American Council on Education and Macmillan, 1986.

Vaughan, G. B. *Leadership in Transition.* New York: American Council on Education and Macmillan, 1989.

Susan B. Twombly is assistant professor of higher education in the Department of Educational Policy and Administration at the University of Kansas, Lawrence.

The development of a career within one institution calls for conscious planning and the development of skills and strategies that may differ from those typically exhibited in an interinstitutional career.

Thriving at Home: Developing a Career as an Insider

Mary Ann D. Sagaria, Cynthia S. Dickens

Imbedded within the common myths and over-the-counter advice about administrative advancement in higher education is the assumption that career advancement is largely a consequence of mobility between institutions. Yet, observers of higher education administrators are more often struck by the single-institution steadfastness of administrative careers rather than by their institutional mobility. The majority of higher education administrators, like most managers and professionals in profit and nonprofit organizations, build their careers in one or two organizations (Moore, 1983). This does not mean that they are not marketable beyond their home institutions. Many are recruited by and explore options in other organizations each year but find it more desirable to remain in their "home" institutions. Others may have anticipated greater career mobility but find that changes in economic conditions or family responsibilities have increased the financial and psychological costs of reestablishing their homes and careers. The conclusion that we can draw from their experiences is clear: Regardless of what administrators plan or anticipate for their future work lives, prospects are very good that each will remain affiliated with a single organization. Therefore, thinking about a career in one institution is not only meaningful but also increasingly imperative.

We approach career development as a dynamic process in which individuals make environmental and personal assessments moving toward a "fit" or congruence between their work and themselves. A career is a

We acknowledge the helpful comments of Gay B. Hadley, Nancy K. Campbell, and James R. Tootle in preparing this chapter.

long-term work history that displays an "intended and intentional sense of direction which honors aspects of one's personal life" (Derr, 1986, p. ix). It is not defined by title changes or progress up a fictional ladder. Thus, career success is being able both to live out the values in which one believes and to make contributions to the world of work (Derr, 1986). The development of a career within one institution calls for conscious planning and the development of skills and strategies that may differ from those typically exhibited in a career characterized by movement between institutions (Twombly, 1988). The literature on administrative careers has emphasized mobility across institutions. Consequently, there is little empirical data available to shed light on the ways in which careers within one higher education institution are developed. It is clear, however, that insiders—those individuals who are accepted as members of the organization and who have special knowledge of its affairs or are able to influence its decisions—exhibit a range of professional skills and personal qualities that are valued by their home institutions, and that they devise effective career strategies.

In this chapter we draw upon our insights into the workings of academic organizations, our scholarship, and our observations of insiders in order to (1) recognize and encourage career growth within a home institution and (2) to increase awareness of organizational realities that can expand career options and provide opportunities. For those individuals who carefully plan careers as well as for those who prefer careers that evolve serendipitously, these considerations lead to our five propositions for "thriving at home," that is, developing a successful career within one institution.

Proposition 1

In order to recognize and prepare for career opportunities, the insider must understand the complex nature of higher education institutions. Colleges and universities tend to reward and rely on people who have worked well for them in the past. They are conservative organizations that attempt to minimize internal uncertainty and environmental risk. In the language of open systems theory, universities attempt to maintain steady states, or the condition of homeostasis. The less disruption the system experiences, the fewer resources or less energy it uses to restore its equilibrium (Bolman and Deal, 1984). Institutions of higher education attempt to anticipate the unforeseen and to control its impact. By evaluating past achievements and retaining and motivating employees, they reduce the likelihood of disruptions in their traditional patterns of thinking and acting.

Under adverse conditions, organizations discover efficiencies that they previously ignored (March, 1982). Although adversity also offers the opportunity to develop new strategies and to relinquish old identities and behaviors that may be maladaptive to new environmental conditions (Alpert, 1985; Morgan, 1986), the normative institutional response is to perform the old tasks in more efficient ways, to focus on internal economies rather than external conditions. The insider can use conditions of adversity as an opportunity to contribute to the organization by serving on a cost-containment committee, for example, or by proposing strategies to offset an unfavorable situation. The insider who accepts new assignments or takes on an additional responsibility assists the organization while demonstrating versatility, breadth, and sensitivity to organizational needs. Moreover, the institution that reorganizes or promotes an insider whose work quality, attitudes, and loyalties are known can conserve scarce resources and eliminate the risk attendant to bringing in an outsider.

Because academic institutions are complex and conservative, they change slowly. Most significant and enduring changes that occur in colleges and universities result from an almost imperceptible evolutionary process. Although the catalyst for change may come from a variety of sources, including a new president, his or her cabinet members, or technological advances, the institution's responses are shaped by the collective will and interests of its career employees through informal as well as formal groups and processes. The implementation of new policies and procedures requires the support and cooperation of a core of influential and loyal administrative, faculty, and professional staff members. Thus, insiders need to anticipate and attempt to influence rather than impede or resist change. Also, they should demonstrate the ability to function effectively within a system of informal networks that is rarely captured by organizational charts. A change in executive leadership, for example, may provide opportunities for the insider to recommend a new student retention program, to participate actively in a capital fund drive, or to campaign for a more environmentally responsive campus.

Proposition 2

In order to understand how to thrive, an insider must be versatile, displaying skills and interests that transcend administrative and functional boundaries and developing an organizationwide network. Furthermore, the insider must develop and apply his or her organizational knowledge to the institution's changing needs and political environment, and he or she must exert influence. An insider's knowledge of a particular organization goes beyond the official rhetoric, formal policies, and even ever-present rumor mills. The insider has knowledge that includes not only an understanding of the rules, values, and norms of the organization but also a sense of its opportunities and constraints. Insider knowledge reveals an understanding of the personnel system, how jobs are created and filled, and who makes key decisions. The insider develops a subjective impression, a "feel" for the institution, for its history and philosophy, and for its members. By participating in the daily life of the organization, attending significant functions such as board of trustees' meetings, discussing with colleagues the implications of events and issues, and articulating well-informed opinions, the insider discovers common interests and forms relationships with members of diverse university constituencies, thereby developing larger networks and identifying opportunities for further participation.

Organizational knowledge also includes the ability to function comfortably in an environment and to know when and where contributions will be most effective. Furthermore, it involves being known and being seen, establishing an institutional reputation and gaining support, recognition, and sponsorship. Versatility is the hallmark of successful careers within one organization. Insiders can use their institutional knowledge to plan career advancement strategies capable of circumventing even the unseen and unexpected barriers that can limit career opportunities in a single administrative area. The faculty member who plans to become a chairperson, associate dean, and then dean within his or her college or the program director who aspires to become dean of students, and then vice-president for student affairs, are likely to find that reorganization, changes in presidential leadership, delays in retirements, and shifts in organizational priorities can undermine career plans. The versatile administrator or faculty member who has learned the politics of the home institution by serving on important committees and who has learned to see problems and issues from an institutional level may discover opportunities where others find barriers.

A viable career strategy for insiders, particularly those in smaller institutions, is to contemplate multiple opportunities within several functional areas such as student affairs, business and finance, and institutional advancement. Although the walls of academic affairs can be impenetrable to the administrator working in student or business affairs, a person who is versatile may be called on to lead in various areas of a university or college. Thus, the assistant dean of an academic college who is particularly effective with students may be tapped to become dean of students, or the associate director of admissions who has organized and promoted a successful orientation program for parents and community leaders may display marketing and communication skills that are rewarded through university advancement. The insider who possesses highly valued, generic, or transferable qualities and who demonstrates expansive thinking rather than tunnel vision may create career opportunities in a variety of functional areas.

Proposition 3

The organizational culture with its norms, values, ideologies, traditions, and institutional memory defines appropriate behaviors for career advancement. The insider must understand and exhibit these behaviors. Within each work setting where there is a definable group with a significant history (Tierney, 1990), a subtle but powerful constellation of symbols, ceremonies, stories, and traditions emerges. These expressive features of a workplace (Clark, 1972) provide meaning and can unite the members of a group. The culture of an organization shapes and limits behavior, provides group members with a sense of identity, and increases organizational stability (Tierney, 1990). The use of language, the allocation of space, and the significance placed on the use of work and personal time all express meaning to the members of a group. Therefore, the format selected for a memo, the selection of one's office location, and the practice of working through the lunch hour are communicative behaviors that either conform to or contradict the accepted norms of a particular institution.

Members of an organization learn and interpret the culture until much of it is taken for granted. Outsiders or new members of the group learn such social understanding slowly, carefully, and strategically, if at all, through sustained contact with insiders until they develop the point of view of insiders (Wilkins and Ouchi, 1983). University or college administrators who understand the culture of their home institutions, who display an understanding of and appreciation for "how we do things around here," are likely to have an advantage over outsiders. Although an understanding of the local culture cannot in itself solve administrative, financial, or academic problems, it is an important prerequisite for insight into organizational opportunities and constraints.

Administrative and professional staff are expected to become attached to the institution, to adapt well to its norms, and to help perpetuate its distinctiveness. Insiders who build careers within a single institution tend to share an "institutional memory" of those strategies that have served the institution well and those that have failed. Clark's (1972) observation regarding the role of faculty also describes frequent role expectations for administrative and professional staff. He notes that believers can become critical in protecting the institution against "later leaders and other new participants who, less pure in belief, might turn the organization in some other direction" (1972, p. 39). The insider who is sensitive to these organizational nuances can avoid the cultural errors often committed by the outsider. Knowing how to dress appropriately, where to sit, what time to arrive for a meeting, or what conversational topics to avoid may on the surface seem inconsequential; however, as subtle as these behaviors may seem to a casual observer, they express meaning and reinforce the values that bind members of the organization together.

Proposition 4

Colleges and universities are social institutions that reflect and perpetuate ideologies that value and advantage some people on the basis of their gender, race, ethnicity, class, age, and sexual orientation. Underrepresented persons must understand and recognize these organizational and individual behaviors and act in a purposeful manner when confronted by them in order to ensure career opportunities. Furthermore, dominant group members must work deliberately to change organizational and individual behaviors to foster a greater acceptance of diversity. American social relations and institutions continue to mirror the values of the dominant race and ethnic group, class, and gender. Despite the existence of antidiscrimination laws, court-mandated desegregation plans, and affirmative action policies, white, middle-class men continue to be disproportionately represented in positions of prestige and power. While the vast majority of college and universities adhere to formal affirmative action policies and procedures and most senior administrators are well intentioned, the slow progress of underrepresented groups indicates that subtle and perhaps unconscious biases and prejudices continue to create barriers and obstacles in college and university life.

Although the number of women employed by colleges and universities is increasing, women administrators are more likely to hold midlevel positions (Sagaria, 1985), and women and minority faculty are more likely to be employed in less prestigious departments and institutions, "concentrated in positions which are perceived as being functionally limited or peripheral to the primary mission of the institution" (Sagaria, Pruitt, and Gagné, 1990, p. 6). Shavlik, Touchton, and Pearson (1990) have noted that salary disparities among men and women holding faculty and administrative positions continue to occur throughout the nation, with disparities greatest at the senior levels but present at entry levels as well.

It is clear that women, nonwhites, and other minority groups bring a variety of skills, socialization experiences, lifestyles, and expectations to the workplace. As career insiders, however, they present the institution with a paradox: They reduce risk because of their insider stature, but they represent increased risk as minority candidates. Although they compete well for midlevel positions that emphasize job-specific skills, they are at a disadvantage for senior-level positions that emphasize such amorphous qualities as competence, "which is inextricably linked with acceptance and enhanced by social similarity or common experience with the normative administrator" (Sagaria, 1985, p. 21). Differences in physical appearance and presentation of self may be perceived as differences in belief systems. Thus, minority insiders may be prejudicially perceived as culturally unacceptable and nonsupportive of the institution's goals and thereby face difficulties in successfully competing with candidates of the dominant group.

Some institutions offer attractive career opportunities to minority candidates, particularly to those insiders with whom the institution is familiar. Indeed, occasionally, a majority group candidate for a position will claim that a minority candidate is advantaged because of his or her race, ethnicity, or gender. However, becoming an insider in the full sense is more difficult for underrepresented persons. They are less likely to "inherit" networks and support groups. They may be confined to faculty or staff positions that are targeted to serve special populations, and they may be overlooked despite their interests in broader areas or their generic skills. Moreover, underrepresented individuals are more likely to be perceived as token members of the organization (Kanter, 1977) rather than as highly qualified, loyal insiders, and they are more likely to be rigorously scrutinized and filtered out of search processes on the basis of personal qualities (Sagaria, Pruitt, and Gagné, 1990). Clearly, insider status by itself does not guarantee fair or preferential treatment. However, the minority insider who displays an understanding of the institution's culture, needs, and means of operation, who has multiple networks and transferable skills, and who presents himself or herself in a manner acceptable to officials making promotion decisions, in effect has devised successful career strategies.

Proposition 5

Colleges and universities offer insiders distinctive opportunities for career advancement through personnel practices that protect and reward current employees and provide opportunities for professional development and advancement. Managing a career necessitates being aware of these opportunities and preparing for and selectively taking advantage of them. Higher education organizations are more likely to promote an insider to an administrative or professional position than to hire an external candidate. Many individual institutions and statewide systems have developed employment policies and procedures intended to benefit current employees. In the State University of New York system, for example, campuses must consider system-internal candidates before external applicants can be formally considered. Other advantageous employment procedures, such as those practiced at Ohio State University, allow a position vacancy to be advertised within the university with a designation that a candidate is under consideration. Sagaria and Johnsrud (1987) revealed that approximately 60 percent of the 2,297 administrative and professional position vacancies at Ohio State University between 1978 and 1985 were filled by insiders, and that over time officials were increasingly likely to select a successful candidate before advertising a position vacancy. By 1985, 65 percent of all internally filled positions were in fact promotions without open searches.

Even among institutions that require open searches, insiders are given opportunities to enhance their competitiveness for vacant positions. They may have chances to perform in new areas, to develop new skills, to enroll in formal degree programs, and to expand their responsibilities. Insiders also may be given sensitive assignments and tested in settings that present minimal risk to the individual or to the organization. They are appointed to assistant, associate, and "acting" positions and often become strong contenders for permanent line appointments. A study of deans in doctorate-granting universities indicated that half of the acting deans were appointed to regular deanships (Sagaria, 1986).

The insider who has developed strong personal and professional ties within the institution and the local community can become an attractive candidate for administrative positions requiring an external community focus. Within community colleges, regional universities, and particularly in academic programs such as business, education, nursing, and fine arts, cultivating community support and gaining access to significant constituencies is a critical administrative job prerequisite. Moreover, the insider's attachments to the community can serve to broaden his or her professional role, increase his or her potential value to the college or university, and personalize the institution in the eyes of the community members.

Professional development opportunities in the form of leadership-training programs and internships are also available to insiders. While year-long and summer programs such as the American Council on Education Fellows Program, the Harvard Institute for Educational Management and the Management Development Program, and the Summer Institute for Women in Higher Education Administration (sponsored by Bryn Mawr College and HERS/Mid-America) may be options for the development of career-enhancing skills, other in-house staff development activities, such as the California State University Administrative Fellows Program and the Committee on Institutional Cooperation Academic Fellows Program, provide opportunities for faculty and administrators to explore their career interests, expand their professional networks, and develop new skills.

Career advancement also can occur through accruing responsibilities (that is, the addition of activities or functions) that eventually lead to the creation of new positions. Accrual mobility occurs when an employee's responsibilities, skills, and knowledge exceed the duties normally assigned to the position, leading to a formal change in the job. Unlike the process of job enrichment, the change is institutionalized through an adjustment in title, salary, or other job features such as staff or budget (Miner and Estler, 1985). "The essential mechanism for accrual mobility is an evolved job, in which the duties were not prespecified independent of the incumbent, rather the duties developed around the activities and/or the abilities of that person" (Miner and Estler, 1985, p. 125). Although a number of individual, organizational, and environmental factors are likely to contribute to accrual mobility, the insider who demonstrates intellectual curiosity, competence, and the ability to influence or change the system may be successful in evolving current responsibilities into a position acknowledged and rewarded by the institution. For example, the financial aid officer who develops effective parent/student counseling programs or the accountant who designs and implements a complex financial forecasting model expand not only their knowledge but also their usefulness to the institution to the extent that new positions are created in order to take advantage of their evolving and salient expertise.

Thus, insiders are offered distinctive career opportunities. Concomitantly, they must be alert to changes within the institution and its environment and be prepared to shape their opportunities. Because colleges and universities are part of a national and international academic community, insiders must make a special effort to be current within their specific professions and disciplines, to be well informed of broader educational, political, economic, and social issues, and to avoid being perceived as narrowly focused, unimaginative, or satisfied with the status quo. Attendance at national conferences, service to professional organizations and boards, and contributions to scholarly journals and professional publications can be professionally and personally rewarding while assuring that the insider maintains a broad perspective on the issues facing the institution.

Implications

There are no guaranteed prescriptions for developing a career as an insider, since no set of provisions will apply to all careers or institutions. Rather, we must develop an understanding of the desired match between our work and ourselves and the possible career directions that emerge from that match. We also must be cognizant of alternative means for designing and managing work changes in an environment that we know well and of which we are very much a part.

Meaningful careers must be a focus of our efforts. Career development within one organization requires ongoing attentiveness to multiple dimensions of our environment such as political processes, institutional culture, and organizational values and needs. Career development also necessitates formal and informal professional networks through which we can develop and influence activities and behaviors to achieve our career goals. It requires an awareness of and attention to the ways in which we are perceived by others in the institution, how we have performed our jobs, the problems we have solved, the ideas we have offered, the issues we have supported, the alliances we have formed, and the images we have created. All of our behaviors become meaningful as they contribute to reputational bases that enable us to develop successful careers within one institution. Career development within one higher education organization does not happen serendipitously. If career development is to occur in a meaningful way, then insiders should expect to become actively involved in the process, accepting responsibility for their own career development and for the development of their college or university.

References

Alpert, D. "Performance and Paralysis: The Organizational Context of the American Research University." *Journal of Higher Education,* 1985, *56,* 241-281.

Bolman, L. G., and Deal, T. E. *Modern Approaches to Understanding and Managing Organizations.* San Francisco: Jossey-Bass, 1984.

Clark, B. R. "The Organizational Saga in Higher Education." *Administrative Science Quarterly*, 1972, 17, 178-184.

Derr, C. B. *Managing the New Careerists: The Diverse Career Success Orientations of Today's Workers.* San Francisco: Jossey-Bass, 1986.

Kanter, R. M. *Men and Women of the Corporation.* New York: Basic Books, 1977.

March, J. G. "Emerging Developments in the Study of Organizations." *Review of Higher Education*, 1982, 6 (1), 1-17.

Miner, A. S., and Estler, S. E. "Accrual Mobility: Job Mobility in Higher Education Through Responsibility Accrual." *Journal of Higher Education*, 1985, 56, 121-143.

Moore, K. M. *Leaders in Transition: A National Study of Higher Education Administrators.* University Park: Center for the Study of Higher Education, The Pennsylvania State University, 1983.

Morgan, G. *Images of Organization.* Newbury Park, Calif.: Sage, 1986.

Sagaria, M.A.D. "The Managerial Skills and Experiences of Men and Women Administrators: Similarities and Differences." *Journal of Educational Equity and Leadership*, 1985, 5 (1), 19-30.

Sagaria, M.A.D. "Deanship Selection: Connections and Consequences." Paper presented at the annual meeting of the American Educational Research Association, San Francisco, April 1986.

Sagaria, M.A.D., and Johnsrud, L. K. *Many Are Candidates, But Few Compete: The Impact of Internal Promotion Change of Administrators and Professional Staff on White Women and Minorities.* Columbus: Department of Educational Policy and Leadership, Ohio State University, 1987.

Sagaria, M.A.D., Pruitt, A. S., and Gagné, P. L. *Enhancing Administrative Recruitment of Minorities and Women at The Ohio State University.* Columbus: Department of Educational Policy and Leadership, Ohio State University, 1990.

Shavik, D. L., Touchton, J. G., and Pearson, C. S. "The New Agenda of Women for Higher Education." In C. S. Pearson, D. L. Shavlik, and J. G. Touchton (eds.), *Educating the Majority: Women Challenge Tradition in Higher Education.* New York: American Council on Education and Macmillan, 1990.

Tierney, W. G. *Curricular Landscapes, Democratic Vistas: Transformative Leadership in Higher Education.* New York: Praeger, 1990.

Twombly, S. B. "Administrative Labor Markets: A Test of the Existence of Internal Labor Markets in Two-Year Colleges." *Journal of Higher Education*, 1988, 59, 668-689.

Wilkins, A. L., and Ouchi, W. G. "Efficient Cultures: Exploring the Relationship Between Culture and Organizational Performance." *Administrative Science Quarterly*, 1983, 28, 468-481.

Mary Ann D. Sagaria is associate professor in the Department of Educational Policy and Leadership at Ohio State University, Columbus.

Cynthia S. Dickens is vice-president for student affairs at Northern Kentucky University, Highland Heights.

The Chronicle of Higher Education *is full of advertisements for academic administrators. How does an individual sort out the realities of a particular search? What can be learned from hiring practices and procedures?*

Lessons in Hiring Practices for Aspiring Academic Administrators

Michael R. Dingerson

Those of us currently aspiring to academic administrative positions are encountering substantially different conditions and behaviors in higher education than those who pursued such positions prior to 1972. It was then that the *Higher Education Guidelines Executive Order 11246* (U.S. Department of Health, Education, and Welfare, 1972) was implemented, calling for an expanded recruitment effort with the intent of employing more individuals from underrepresented populations. Subsequent actions have modified this original effort in significant ways. Today, most colleges and universities follow fairly similar policies and procedures to fill positions.

What then has replaced the "old boy" network, if anything, in the hiring process? How can one understand better what is happening or likely to happen in a given hiring activity related to a specific position at a specific institution? Are there ways to gain insights into these issues from secondary information? How can one optimize the likelihood of making the "final cut," receiving an interview, and getting an offer for a position?

There are few substitutes for good experience and high-quality academic credentials for gaining a desired position. However, there are also lessons to be learned from the literature and from those with substantial hiring experience in academic administration settings. The purpose of this chapter is to explore these issues with the expectation that those job candidates who are more informed about these concerns will be more likely to seek out realistic opportunities and ultimately will be more successful in building their administrative careers. Such issues as knowing when and when not to apply, understanding others' experiences in moving up and down the "institution-type" ladder, knowing the backgrounds of successful applicants for similar positions, interpreting advertising behaviors, and knowing what the literature has to say about the ways specific types of positions are filled are all important to a candidate's successful participation in a job search.

Knowing One's Boundaries

Much of what is presented in the following few paragraphs is obvious, yet it is surprising how many candidates who apply for administrative positions are simply not qualified for one reason or another. My experience is that well over 50 percent of the applicants for any single position are not qualified. Why, then, do they apply? Is it reasonable for these individuals to take the attitude: "What will it hurt. No one will ever know?" Or could there be damaging consequences from such action?

I believe very strongly that the latter case is more valid. Administrative and institutional spheres are simply too connected for word not to get around. No one will criticize others for seeking a position for which they are qualified, but unqualified candidates will damage their reputations in making unwarranted applications. The thinking goes something like this: "If they think they are qualified for this position when most of their colleagues do not, what other 'out of touch' behaviors might they exhibit, and how dependable would they be in a position for which they are qualified?"

It is unwise for anyone to raise these kinds of questions by applying for that out-of-reach opportunity and possibly hindering the pursuit of positions for which he or she is qualified. How does an individual know for sure about whether or not to apply? One way is to ask a trusted senior person to provide an assessment. Another is to find a person in a similar position and ask what kinds of credentials and experiences are considered valuable in filling that type of position.

Institution Type and Position Match

Just as an individual in a community college usually would not be a serious candidate for a substantial academic administrative position in a research university, the reverse also holds true. Each type of institution has a purpose, mission, and culture to consider when making hiring decisions, and few are likely to take the gamble of hiring someone considered to be "outside their element."

How do we know, then, what defines our appropriate "institutional element"? Most job mobility occurs across similar types of institutions. Further, many people believe that it is much easier to move to a "lesser" institution than to a "greater" one. It is also generally understood that an individual can move down two levels in terms of type of institution and yet move up substantially in terms of the nature and prestige of the position. Moving back up the institutional ladder, however, is very difficult if not impossible.

These general circumstances make the type of institution of paramount importance. It is rather like the "big fish in a small pond or small fish in a big pond" notion. One must choose with great care and diligence the type of institution with which to be associated. Occasionally, an individual can move up the institution-type ladder. I will never forget the reaction from a colleague upon learning the identity of the previous institution of a person filling a major academic position on a Big Ten campus: "Wyoming!? Wyoming!? We've hired a vice-president from Wyoming!!??" His incredulity said it all. However, there are at least two facts of significance in this example. The first is the shock of my colleague. The second is the success of the candidate in question in securing the position—evidence that people actually do move up the ladder on occasion.

Sources of Successful Applicants

This area has two dimensions: traditional versus nontraditional and internal versus external sources. Socolow (1978, p. 42) noted that "higher education in the country, and in this half of the decade, is plagued by dramatically declining enrollments, increasingly disparate student clienteles, and serious fiscal crises." He also said that under the circumstances, "one would surely expect to see some experimentation taking the form of recruitment and hiring of key people with special skills in managing institutions during troubled times" (1978, p. 42). One of his basic questions was, "Are there trends in hiring that deviate from past practice?" That is, he was looking for deviations from the following: "Senior positions in academic administration have long been the almost exclusive province of those who have served for a substantial time in academe, moving from one rung of the ladder to the next—most often from professor to chairman to dean to vice president to president" (1978, p. 42). Drawing from information appearing in the "Bulletin Board" section of the *Chronicle of Higher Education,* Socolow (1978, p. 42) concluded that "the most striking finding of the study was the clear persistence of all the institutions in drawing only from a traditional pool of candidates."

In general, my own experience confirms this conclusion, with one possible exception. Since hiring practices have remained rather constant in terms of the nature of the search and, more important, in terms of those individuals who make the hiring decisions, there is little reason to believe that the type of individual hired has changed or is changing much in academic administration. The one exception is at the presidential level. Given the new and expanding responsibilities that exist for the chief operating officer, boards of trustees have demonstrated more of a tendency to hire "nontraditional" presidents than in the past. Examples abound of the lawyer, businessman (almost always "man"), or politician who was hired, much to the chagrin of faculty members and others who expect a traditional academic to become president.

The aspiring academic administrator, however, is not usually seeking a presidential position. The lesson to be gleaned from the traditional versus nontraditional issue is that academic experience is the best credential even if it is not always required. Implicit in the progression from professor to dean to vice-president is the fact that individuals pay their dues by progressing through the ranks to full professorships. Occasionally, that sequence is not necessary for entry-level positions such as assistant and associate administrators. Frequently, in fact, these entry-level positions are used to groom people for higher academic administrative careers and are available to those who are at an advanced, assistant professor level or who have been promoted to associate professorships. There is just no doubt that the single most important issue for successful aspirants to academic administrative positions is the quality of their academic experience. Promotion to full professor is almost always a requirement for successful dean candidates as well as for successful department chair candidates on many campuses.

Substantial data are available from 1972 onward to demonstrate significant changes in hiring of external versus internal applicants. There is also evidence to indicate that these data vary little by types of positions when considering only line positions. Glennen and McCollough (1976), Hutchison and Johnson (1980), Dingerson, Rodman, and Burns (1985), and Johnson and Hutchison (1990) have studied trends in internal versus external sources of successful candidates since the 1972 federal guidelines (U.S. Department of Health, Education, and Welfare, 1972). This research attempts to discover if there have been significant changes over time in terms of more candidates coming from sources external to the hiring institutions. To one degree or another, all have supported the notion that the greater percentage of academic administrators hired come from external sources.

With the exception of Glennen and McCollough (1976), the other researchers addressed the internal versus external issue longitudinally. Two studies cover 1972–1979 and one covers 1972–1989. Since Hutchison and Johnson (1980) and Johnson and Hutchison (1990) used the same data for 1972 and 1979, these data allow only a single comparison with the Dingerson, Rodman, and Burns (1985) data. The Johnson and Hutchison (1990) data allow an inspection of continuation or decline of the previous trend. Essentially, even though the data of each study are not directly comparable, it is clear (especially from Johnson and Hutchison, 1990) that there was a dramatic shift from internal to external sources of successful candidates from 1972 to 1979. In 1972, 60 percent were hired from inside. That condition had reversed by 1979 with 65 percent hired from outside. By 1984, nearly 75 percent of the successful candidates were hired from external sources. These data are very consistent by year and type of position being studied: academic vice-presidents, deans, and department chairs.

Position Advertisements

Are there lessons to be learned from the pattern of job advertisements for academic administrative positions? I believe there are. According to Dingerson, Rodman, and Burns (1985), the number of advertisements increased substantially after the 1972 federal guidelines (U.S. Department of Health, Education, and Welfare, 1972) were put in place. Using the *Chronicle of Higher Education* as the source of data, the number of advertisements more than doubled between 1973 and 1976. Obviously, this was in response to the notion that institutions must advertise nationally if they truly seek underrepresented individuals for traditional positions. After 1976, the level of advertising dropped in what has been identified as an anomalous year, 1977, and then increased to about the 1976 level by 1979 (Dingerson, Rodman, and Burns, 1985, p. 119).

Obviously, increases alone in the level of advertising would not necessarily result in the hiring of greater numbers of underrepresented individuals, nor would they signify fair search and hiring processes. We need to look deeper into the data to better understand what is occurring in the hiring process.

Advertising behavior may or may not predictably indicate what is actually intended in a particular search. While there are no certain telltale signs, there may be clues in the advertisements themselves and in advertising practices, for example, the number of times an advertisement is placed and in what and how many locations. We need to face the fact that some searches are destined from the beginning to result in the hiring of individuals already identified and favored for the advertised positions. Unfortunately, those kinds of bogus searches entice many unknowing individuals, occupy the time of their references, and generally create a credibility problem for the institutions involved. There are also searches that are conducted fairly, with open attempts to find the best candidates, but that still result in the hiring of the "obvious" candidates. These kinds of searches are frequently criticized as being "wired from the start." Since there are only two options in placing an advertisement for an available position, to advertise nationally or locally, there are few ways of avoiding being the "innocent" candidate in a search that is essentially destined to hire a specific person. Since a full search procedure is required to fill most, if not all, positions, what can a potential candidate learn from the frequency and location of advertisements?

My advice is to beware of any position advertised at the national level in only one outlet and for only one time. Although this warning may not always provide an accurate interpretation of specific situations (suggestions on how to find out are addressed below), it is reasonable to assume from this information that there is an intended candidate for the position. Before hiring that individual, under most institutional personnel and affirmative action policies, a national search has to be conducted. Placing an advertisement once, in the *Chronicle of Higher Education*, for example, would meet that requirement. The potential candidate needs to be very cautious about making absolute interpretations on this matter, however, for there could be other reasons for this type of advertising behavior. For instance, an institution that funds position advertisements from a central budget may have a policy that limits the number of times an advertisement can be run. More frequently, however, each hiring unit is responsible for these expenses. So useful information can be garnered by studying advertising practices, and when it seems wise, asking questions.

Positions advertised only locally are usually destined to be filled in one of two ways. First, there is either an intended or at least a "safe" candidate available who would be satisfactory for the position if a better candidate did not surface. Second, there is not a favored candidate available and the attitude is "there are lots of good candidates out there so let's advertise locally and see who's interested." The latter type of situation bodes well for qualified candidates seeking entry-level positions. These positions are frequently staff positions, sometimes intended as "grooming" experiences for future academic administrators. But again I must stress that there are no absolutes in interpreting these situations. It is important to assess specific cases carefully and to draw conclusions cautiously.

The research of Dingerson, Rodman, and Wade (1980, 1982) and Dingerson, Rodman, and Burns (1985) found a correlation between the actual number of positions available of a certain type and the level of advertising, thus illustrating the type of information that can be gained from observing advertising patterns. This research explored several issues related to hiring practices and costs by focusing on four types of academic administrative positions: chief academic officers, assistant and associate chief academic officers, deans, and assistant and associate deans. The major difference between this work and other studies (for example, Johnson and Hutchison, 1990) is that assistant and associate positions were included. Almost all research in this general area focuses on the line positions of chair, dean, vice-president, and president. Yet, the staff positions may provide critically important avenues to eventual line responsibility. For those with no academic administrative experience, the staff opportunity may be the most viable option available.

Dingerson, Rodman, and Burns (1985) found that different types of positions correlate with different levels of nationally placed advertisements. According to the authors, "If all available positions were being advertised nationally and the chief academic officer position were used as a base of projection, we would expect to find advertisements for an estimated 452 assistant/associate chief academic officers, 1,356 academic deans, and 2,712 assistant/associate academic deans in the sample rather than the actually requested figures of 50, 376, and 57, respectively" (1985, p. 131). The projections were made by assuming a ratio of 1:2 for chief academic officers to assistant and associate chief academic officers, a ratio of 1:6 for chief academic officers to academic deans, and a ratio of 1:2 for academic deans to assistant and associate academic deans.

These data seem to indicate that of the three positions below the chief academic officer position, the dean position is most likely to be advertised on a national basis. Although it is possible that the other positions are being advertised in other ways, it is highly unlikely that any organization serious about attracting a competitive, external pool of candidates from a national search would not advertise in the *Chronicle of Higher Education*. These data also may suggest that any assistant or associate position advertised nationally is most likely the result of a search in which the institution is committed to finding an external candidate. The fact that relatively few assistant and associate positions are advertised nationally indicates that there are not or may not be qualified or acceptable candidates within the institutions. Since these positions are often only advertised locally and filled from within, a candidate can better judge his or her best chance at being successful in pursuing one of these positions by studying an institution's advertising behavior.

Sorting Out the Facts

Let us assume that potential candidates notice an advertisement in the *Chronicle of Higher Education* for a dean position. How do they learn more about this particular search? First, they should determine if the position has been advertised in other national publications, and, if so, in which ones. If the position is advertised in one or more national publications, there is reason to believe that this institution is genuinely interested in attracting as good a candidate pool as possible. Next, they should note where these advertisements have been placed. For instance, it is reasonable to conclude that an advertisement placed in *Black Issues in Higher Education* or other minority publications is evidence that the institution is attempting to meet the intent and spirit of the 1972 federal guidelines and is serious about attracting underrepresented individuals to the institution.

Another way to judge more closely what an institution is trying to accomplish with a particular position advertisement is to assess the outlet of the advertisement in terms of preferred academic background of candidates. For instance, if an advertisement for a dean of liberal arts and sciences appears in *Science* but not in comparable journals or other outlets in the arts, humanities, and social sciences, there may be an explicit message being transmitted. Or, if there are two relatively distinct responsibilities combined within a single advertised position, potential candidates should sort out which aspect of the position appears to be most important to the institution. A common position with such dual characteristics is vice-president for research combined with dean of the graduate school. Close inspection of the advertisement helps one discern the sort of credentials and experiences the institution is seeking. For instance, if the intent of the position is more toward the research direction, the advertisement will be biased in that regard and will frequently have absolute requirements in terms of previous responsibilities and time-in-rank. If the intent is toward the graduate administration direction, there will be statements about expanding programs and improving the quality of graduate offerings. Requisite experience in this regard is likely to be noted.

Finally, after collecting and interpreting all available printed information, how do potential applicants learn more without endangering their candidacies? It is usually as simple as asking. Hiring activities on a campus are generally well understood by a broad array of individuals, depending on the position being filled. If a candidate is unfamiliar with a particular campus, there are undoubtedly individuals on the candidate's campus who know to whom questions can be directed. Chairs of similar departments know chairs and other individuals across the country, as do deans. At the institutional level, particularly across like-types of institutions, individuals tend to know each other very well. These networks are very rich sources of important and usually accurate information.

What does the phenomenon of "search reopened" mean for an unsuccessful candidate? This is a "do your homework" issue. If an individual was a candidate for the position in the previous search, chances are he or she will not be a successful candidate for the new search. It is important to find out why the earlier search was not successful. If it was a matter of academic background, that issue is not likely to change. For instance, an academic vice-presidential candidate with the same or a similar disciplinary background as the president may be at a disadvantage. Or, a dean of liberal arts candidate may suffer the "we don't want any more chemists in this role" phenomenon of a particular institution. It is hard, if not impossible, to know about these issues without asking informed individuals. The reverse circumstance is possible also. An individual's academic background can make him or her a more highly regarded candidate. Either instance provides important information to the potential candidate.

How does one assess the "acting" capacity of the incumbent? Is this search just a legitimizing effort to put the acting person in the position permanently? That is a very high possibility. In general, people on campus will know. Sometimes the acting person has informed local sources that he or she is not a candidate. If, however, that person is a declared candidate, the issue becomes much more complex. This sort of situation generally plays out in rather absolute terms. That is, the acting candidate is either very acceptable for the permanent position or very unacceptable. Discreet inquiries frequently result in accurate information in this regard.

There are other institutional variables that come into play in filling a position. Are there any minority chairs or deans? If not, candidates should be aware that a priority in the hiring decision may be ethnic or racial diversity. This factor does not necessarily determine the eventual decision, but all other variables being equal, the hiring of an underrepresented individual is probable. Again, candidates should ask around. Individuals on campus will know if "we need to hire a woman (minority) dean."

It is not unusual to get "mixed messages" when seeking information from a variety of sources. This is a situation that ultimately only the candidate can resolve. My recommendation (assuming candidates are qualified for a position) is to weigh all available information and to proceed positively if the balance sheet appears more positive than negative. There is obviously much more to the hiring process than appears on the surface. An individual who understands these issues will have a better opportunity for a successful outcome.

References

Dingerson, M. R., Rodman, J. A., and Burns, D. "The Hiring of Under-Represented Individuals in Academic Administrative Positions: 1972–1979." *Research in Higher Education,* 1985, *23* (2), 115–134.

Dingerson, M. R., Rodman, J. A., and Wade, J. F. "The Hiring of Academic Administrators Since the 1972 *Higher Education Guidelines.*" *Research in Higher Education,* 1980, *13* (1), 9–22.

Dingerson, M. R., Rodman, J. A., and Wade, J. F. "Procedures and Costs for Hiring Academic Administrators." *Journal of Higher Education,* 1982, *53* (1), 63–74.

Glennen, R. E., and McCollough, J. B. "Selection Trends in College Administrative Positions." *Education,* 1976, *96,* 384–387.

Johnson, A. E., Jr., and Hutchison, J. E. "Executive Order 11246 and the Demographics of Academic Administrators." *Journal of the College and University Personnel Association,* 1990, *41* (1), 19–23.

Hutchison, J. E., and Johnson, A. E., Jr. "Demographic Changes in Administrative Appointees." *Journal of the College and University Personnel Association,* 1980, *31* (2), 31–36.

Socolow, D. J. "How Administrators Got Their Jobs." *Change,* 1978, *10* (5), 42–54.

U.S. Department of Health, Education, and Welfare. Office for Civil Rights. *Higher Education Guidelines Executive Order 11246.* Washington, D.C.: Government Printing Office, 1972.

Michael R. Dingerson is associate vice-chancellor for research and dean of the graduate school and professor of higher education at the University of Mississippi, University.

Searches are highly situational, rarely rational processes.

Encountering Search Committees

Jane Fiori Lawrence, Theodore J. Marchese

Looking for a new job is all too often an anxiety-producing, frustrating experience. For those of us who have chosen administrative careers in higher education, the search for a new position is made even more complex by the nature of the selection process, which is committee-driven, time consuming, and often inscrutable. Horror stories abound about shabby treatment of candidates and search committees gone awry.

The goal of this chapter is to help candidates better manage the search process and their interactions with search committees. From the beginning we offer this caveat: Searches are highly situational, rarely rational processes. Their character varies sharply across institution types and administrative fields. Even within the same institution, search committees come in many configurations. One committee will be cohesive, well led, and fully ready for the complexity of the search process; the next may be deeply split over campus priorities, have an ineffectual chair, and be unprepared for the demands of a proper search.

So there are few rules and no simple guidelines that apply to every situation a candidate encounters. Given campus politics, internal candidacies, vagaries of the applicant pool, and the unpredictable nature of committees, a candidate's ability to predict or control events is inherently limited.

Maria Perez (Marchese, 1989, p. 3), an executive recruiter specializing in higher education, notes that "search committees are strange creatures . . . often they don't really know what they are looking for. . . . Committees define what they are looking for as they begin to see resumés, even as they interview people, and they keep redefining it. Sometimes an individual walks in and he or she completely changes the definition and gets the job. *So never assume you are in a process that is clear-cut and rational*" (emphasis

New Directions for Higher Education, no. 72, Winter 1990 © Jossey-Bass Inc., Publishers

added). Despite these caveats, candidates can improve their chances of impressing a search committee by careful preparation. This chapter reviews some of the latest thinking by search experts on how candidates can best position themselves for success.

Preparation

If an individual is about to enter the administrative job market, either for the first time or for the sake of career advancement, the first step is to get a feel for the range and types of jobs that are available. At this stage, the individual should think expansively. "Are there new positions of interest or fields of work I would like to enter? A part of the country that I wish to live in? A type of institution that I prefer to work at? Am I looking for a promotion or a lateral move?" The *Chronicle of Higher Education* remains the best, single place to look for job openings in higher education. It is important to read through the advertisements in several issues to get a sense of the kinds of positions available and what qualifications institutions claim they want. An individual should examine his or her professional background and qualifications realistically but not prematurely rule out a long-shot application or two. As a friend of ours is fond of saying, "Don't turn down any jobs that haven't been offered yet to you or someone else."

Most search specialists recommend that when a person is ready to enter the job market, he or she should apply for *several* positions simultaneously—not just one, and certainly not one hundred. Any single application is always a long shot; one hundred "canned" applications have a near-zero chance of success. It is reasonable to apply for four to eight positions, each carefully chosen (attractive post, viable candidacy) and each carefully pursued (more on this in a moment).

Parenthetically, we do not think it is ethical to apply for positions that one would not take if offered. If an individual's spouse is ensconced in a position in Florida and resistant to moving, there is no reason to apply for that job in Oregon unless the couple is considering a commuter marriage, which, of course, some people do. The individual should save his or her own time and the committee's for serious applications.

When applying for positions, an important early task is to find out as much as possible about those institutions and posts. The applicant should call each admissions office and ask for a catalog and other promotional materials, contact colleagues who teach or work at the place, speak with friends who live in the area about community perceptions of the institution, and check out the campus in guidebooks and higher education directories. It is also important to try to discover what issues are currently under debate on that campus: Are faculty or administrators worried about undergraduate education, relations with the legislature, or a decline in research grants? Are staff and faculty disaffected from the administration? If so, why? If a particular personal interest or commitment such as student community-service activities will affect the decision to apply, the applicant should find out if that is a priority on the campus in question.

All of this effort has a purpose: to help determine whether the opening warrants pursuit, and (if it does) to help place the best possible application before the search committee. If the decision is made to go forward, the intelligence gathering done beforehand becomes the foundation for the subsequent letter of application, contacts with the chair, and conversations with the search committee.

Self-Presentation

The one part of the search process that candidates can control is how they present themselves in contacts with the committee, both in writing and in person. Perez (Marchese, 1989) believes that candidates need to manage what the search committee sees. Three points of contact through which they can influence committee perceptions are their cover letters and resumés, their references, and how they prepare for and handle the campus visit.

Cover Letters and Resumés. Most higher education job advertisements—whether in the *Chronicle of Higher Education,* the *New York Times,* a local newspaper, or passed along from a friend—ask for a cover letter and a resumé or curriculum vitae (CV). Armed with the information collected about the campus, the potential candidate should read the advertisement carefully, looking for key words and phrases that indicate the type of personal background and experience that the committee is seeking. If the advertisement reads (as one recently did in the *Chronicle of Higher Education*), "Requirements include a master's degree, a minimum of five years' experience involving significant advisory and managerial responsibility as registrar or associate registrar, a sound working knowledge of on-line student information systems, the ability to deal with a diverse community of faculty, students, parents, and colleagues, and a sensitivity to the goals of independent research universities," then the cover letter should address in a clear, confident, concise manner how one's own preparation and skills match up with these requirements.

The CV or resumé submitted should, of course, be up-to-date. For an initial application, the candidate need not send a full vitae; a summary CV, four to five pages long, is usually adequate for first contacts with an institution. With a personal computer it becomes possible to tailor one's resumé to the job's apparent requirements, emphasizing experience and skills that correspond to what the institution is seeking. (This customization of letters and resumés takes time, a prime reason for limiting the number of applications submitted.)

In all written communications with the committee, appearance, format, and writing style are important. The cover letter and CV should be neat, uncrowded, and easily read. And the applicant should send the committee only those documents that it has requested, retaining articles or statements of philosophy until the committee requests them.

Often candidates wonder if it is better to apply for the position directly or to be nominated. Our advice is to use a nominator only under the following conditions: The nominator is well regarded in his or her field and a person whose judgment will command committee respect; and the nominator knows the candidate well and can speak persuasively about his or her ability to perform in the position. If a colleague is asked to serve as a nominator, it is important to provide him or her with a copy of the CV and a paragraph or two that describes one's qualifications for the post— the latter as a courtesy, but in a spirit also of managing as many parts of the process as possible.

Once the documents are before the committee, the candidate should stay in contact with the chair and respond to any requests, but do so without becoming a nuisance. Higher education searches proceed at their own pace. At this stage in the process, patience is the virtue to cultivate.

As they wait, candidates often worry about the confidentiality of their applications. In sunshine states where all searches are open, candidates know that every application becomes part of the public record. Even in nonsunshine states, confidentiality often proves difficult to maintain. If it is important that the application is kept confidential, the candidate should say so in the cover letter and provide the search committee with a home address and phone number. But leaks can and do occur! Given this risk, the candidate needs to weigh when and how to inform his or her supervisor (and officemates) about the application. At the next stages of calls to references and the campus visit, one's candidacy will not remain secret for long.

References. A second part of the search process over which the candidate can exercise some control is the reference checking that the committee will do. At some point during the search, the candidate will undoubtedly be asked to provide letters of recommendation or the names of colleagues who can comment on his or her qualifications. To the extent possible, it is important to choose people who will command a committee's respect and who know the candidate well and have worked with him or her recently. If the candidate provides the committee with names, these individuals should be given copies of the position description, information on the institution, and the resumé and cover letter. The candidate may ask references to emphasize particular aspects of his or her background related to the post's responsibilities. If asked to send letters of recommendation, the candidate again should provide these references with materials about the job and personal qualifications in order to assist them in writing strong letters.

Campus Visits. If invited to campus to interview for the position, once again preparation is the key. The candidate should ask the chair of the search committee for any additional background materials that might be useful. Before a schedule for the visit is set, the chair should be apprised of any personal needs (for example, a rest period) and preferences (for example, to see a certain vice-president); after the schedule is set, the candidate should ask for the names and titles of the people with whom he or she will be meeting. If expected to make a formal presentation, the candidate should request details relevant to the preparation.

Prior to visiting the campus, it is important to study the materials gathered earlier and perhaps do further intelligence gathering. The candidate should also prepare and practice answers to the questions that undoubtedly will be asked: "Why do you want this position? What special knowledge or abilities will you bring to it? What are your limitations? What are your long-term career goals?" An understanding of the committee's perspective is also important: "If I were on this search committee—as faculty, staff, or student—what questions would I want answered?" Moreover, if the candidate will meet with the appointing officer to whom the committee reports, it is wise to anticipate his or her concerns. Recently, we observed a search where the appointing officer prepared a trick question for the finalists for a senior administrative position. Only one candidate had prepared thoroughly enough to answer the question about the long-term consequences of the post's chief responsibilities. It is not surprising that he was the successful candidate.

Conventional wisdom among search professionals is that the first five minutes of an interview are the most crucial in creating impressions in committee members' minds. (Some experts feel that impressions formed in the first ten seconds can be lasting!) For initial impressions that are positive, matters of entry into the room, posture, and greeting count, as does attire (for example, neat, clean, comfortable clothing that fits well). The candidate's goal is to look as if he or she belongs on that campus.

In interviews, search committees are impressed by the applicant who has read carefully the materials provided and has come prepared to answer tough questions. Nothing seems to turn off a committee faster than an applicant who is "arrogant," or who acts as if he or she has already identified the institution's problems and decided on the solutions.

The applicant must listen carefully to committee questions and offer thoughtful, brief answers. It is important to convey genuine interest in the position and campus, while not appearing "too eager." During the interviews, especially the initial ones, the applicant and the committee are looking for areas of mutual interest and fit. As such, the applicant should not hesitate to ask questions, the more substantive and thoughtful the better. Realistically, though, on an initial visit the committee's needs take precedence, so the applicant should go lightly at this stage with his or her own questions.

Interviewing effectively is a skill that can be learned. There are many good books available to help applicants refine or improve their abilities in this area. At the end of this chapter, we list a few books that should help applicants prepare for these critical encounters with search committees.

Upon returning home, the applicant may want to send thank-you notes to the search committee chair, to committee members who took an unusual interest in his or her candidacy, and to other key individuals encountered during the visit. More than etiquette, these notes are an opportunity to create positive impressions in the minds of committee members.

Getting Answers

As the search proceeds, the committee chair becomes the main contact point with the institution. He or she is a pivotal person in the search, representing simultaneously the views of the appointing officer and the desires of the committee. As circumstances permit, the candidate should work to develop a good relationship with the chair.

During the initial campus visit, the candidate should try to obtain information useful to an evaluation of the position and his or her true interest in it. The goals here are to discover if there is a fit between one's aims and qualifications and the needs of the campus, and to decide if the opportunity is worth pursuing. An important point to remember about getting one's own questions answered is that timing matters. The first half-hour on campus is not the time to ask about salary, fringe benefits, and a job for one's spouse. Nor should the full committee be questioned about specifics of the post or housing prices in the community. The chair (or appointing officer) is the appropriate source of information about particulars of the post and community, and such questions (which are important) should be left for later stages of a visit.

Generally, after all of the candidates have visited the campus, the search committee meets to agree on a group of finalists to recommend to the appointing officer. At this point, the work of the search committee is just about complete. If the institution is indeed interested in a particular candidate, he or she will be asked back by the appointing officer for a second visit. This is the proper time for the candidate to press for answers to any remaining questions, having by now been thoroughly apprised about salary range, fringe benefits, job responsibilities, and other important aspects of the post. In addition, the candidate should have thought through any other issues that require discussion with the appointing officer. Salary, departmental or unit budget increases, computer equipment, released time for research, starting date, moving expenses, criteria for performance evaluation, and so forth are best negotiated *before* the job is accepted.

Conclusion

When candidates are offered the jobs that they hoped to get, all of their hard work and preparation has paid off. If they are not selected, they should not take the rejection personally. As mentioned earlier, search processes are frequently irrational and highly idiosyncratic. If one job does not materialize, individuals should have applications active in other searches that they can pursue enthusiastically.

It is important to learn from the experience of each search by stepping back and analyzing preparation, contacts with the institution, and interviews. Are there areas in need of refinement or improvement? If brought to campus for an interview, the unsuccessful candidate should telephone the chair at search's end. What weaknesses in candidacy were perceived by the committee? How could the self-presentation have been made stronger?

One way to view searches is as a minimarketing campaign. Instead of marketing a product or service, candidates are marketing themselves. By means of skillful preparation and presentation, they try to impress each search committee and, through it, each institution. If a campaign is successful, an immediate position may result. Even if a given campaign is not initially successful, the candidate's name is known favorably around campus for any future opening that may occur; he or she has developed good relations with search committee members and the chair, who not infrequently can provide an advance start on future searches; and he or she has had an experience that can lead to better self-understanding and professional growth. The next time out, with hard work, good preparation, and a better turn of luck, the position will be offered.

Suggestions for Further Reading

As candidates proceed with their searches for new positions, they may find it helpful to refer to written resources, especially those devoted to specific phases of the search process such as the interview or salary negotiation. Below are some of our favorites.

Chastain, S. *Winning the Salary Game: Salary Negotiation for Women*. New York: Wiley, 1980.

Kline, L., and Feinstein, L. *Career Changing: The Worry-Free Guide*. Boston: Little, Brown, 1982.

McAdam, T. W. *Doing Well by Doing Good: The First Complete Guide to Careers in the Nonprofit Sector*. New York: Penguin, 1988.

Medley, H. A. *Sweaty Palms: The Neglected Art of Being Interviewed*. Belmont, Calif.: Lifetime Learning, 1978.

Yate, M. J. *Knock 'Em Dead with Great Answers to Tough Interview Questions*. Boston: Bob Adams, 1988.

Reference

Marchese, T. J. "Search from the Candidate's Perspective—An Interview with Maria M. Perez." *AAHE Bulletin*, 1989, 42 (4), 3-4.

Jane Fiori Lawrence is assistant director of the honors program at the University of Maryland, College Park.

Theodore J. Marchese is vice-president of the American Association for Higher Education and executive editor of the magazine Change.

Professional development activities are a key way to improve job performance and career potential.

Planning for Career Improvement

Sharon A. McDade

Few institutions do an adequate job of career enhancement or professional development with their administrators. Most people must do this for themselves, but there are important things to consider and numerous choices to be made in crafting a solid set of experiences for oneself.

Considerations for Professional Development

Professional development activities are a key way to improve job performance and career potential. Other strategies of career development, such as finding and building a relationship with a mentor, may be more circumstantial—or just plain luck in terms of being able to link up with someone at a mutually useful time in both careers. But anyone can develop a personal plan for career improvement by taking advantage of the availability of a wide range of professional development programs. Few administrators, whether new managers or old hands, invest the time, interest, or energy to plan and pursue their own personal professional development programs. Yet, the payoffs from developing and pursuing personalized programs can be immense in terms of job enhancement and career advancement.

Professional development planning builds on several considerations: the point one is at in the development of a career, the point one is at in mastering a job, preferred personal learning style, and available professional development activities and programs that match these other considerations.

Many people move into administration for the first time from positions within the same institution; for example, a professor typically becomes a department chair at his or her own institution. Conversely, to move into more senior levels of administration, typically an individual leaves one institution and goes to another. There is learning associated with both forms of entry—initially into administration, into new levels of administration, and into a new institution—which can be facilitated by p⸱⸱⸱⸱ipating in appropriate professional development programs.

After settling into a new job and institution, professional development activities can also be an avenue to explore ways to push the job to new levels of challenge. In this growth phase, an administrator may begin to establish a professional reputation based on expertise acquired from the job; for example, a dean of student affairs who establishes an area of expertise in developing programs to foster better relationships among students on issues of diversity may begin to be sought as a speaker on these topics at other campuses and as a convener of panels at national conventions. As a job is mastered and the details become more manageable, administrators begin to reach out beyond the institution to become active in the higher education community and to build and renew networks. Again, professional development programming provides many venues for this activity.

During the mature stage of a job, an administrator has probably mastered the details and cycles of the job and no longer needs to devote full attention to daily operations. Much can now be delegated to the staff, who have been selected and trained for this purpose by the administrator, leaving more time for planning, integrating programs with other units, and assuming additional responsibilities. During this phase, some administrators begin to feel burnout, especially if major initiatives have taken substantial time and energy. In losing the pressure of daily details, others may find their attention wandering and fill the void by seeking new stimuli to stay engaged and energized. Again, participation in professional development activities can help to address these needs, keep an administrator engaged in and intellectually challenged by the job, and involved in issues of relevance to the job and the institution.

Purposes of Professional Development for a New Administrator

Learning the Job. Many professional development programs are designed to help newcomers learn the details about a particular type of job. In addition to providing information on the basic management skills required for the job, these types of programs also typically provide ample doses of sage advice from others who have served in similar jobs for long periods of time. Their "war stories" can be informative about the challenges yet to come as well as provide perspectives on the long-term cycles of the jobs. Such programs also provide excellent foundations for building networks among administrators in similar jobs.

Learning the Institution. For administrators who begin a new job at a new institution, learning that institution is half of the game in achieving success. Such a move can be doubly difficult if the administrator moved into a different segment of institutions; for example, from a research university to a liberal arts college or from a rural comprehensive college to an urban university. Participation in programs sponsored by the institutional segment associations is useful for getting a take on the issues pertinent to that segment, on the movers and shakers, and on the anticipated long-range challenges. For example, attendance at an annual meeting of the American Association of Community and Junior Colleges gives instant insight into the range of community college issues, the variety of programming in place at these institutions to address these issues, the key players on specific issues, and even the common language and respected books. It is also useful to attend meetings of consortiums or regional organizations in which the institution is a member to get a sense of how sister institutions are dealing with common problems.

Building a Network. An administrator rarely has the time to do thorough, scholarly research on each new issue or problem that arises. Instead, successful administrators do their research over the telephone and through correspondence with their network of contacts at their own institution and throughout the higher education community. Network building is not a passive occupation—few contacts are secured without effort. Instead, one needs to actively build a network of resources. Administrators principally build such networks through interaction with people at meetings, workshops, conventions, and other programs. Most professional development programs design opportunities for network building into their structures. Coffee breaks, small group discussions, and luncheon working sessions are all opportunities to bring program participants together so that they can meet new people and build networks. Those who annually attend a particular convention build networks from the people they regularly see, to the point that they can anticipate who they will see and make preconvention arrangements for discussions on specific topics.

Developing a Theoretical Framework. Most administrative work is hands-on, reactive, detail-oriented, and incremental. It is easy to become so buried in the leaves that one forgets the surrounding forest. Often, administrators become so quickly mired in the details of a project that they never even have the opportunity to think about the theoretical framework in which the project exists. Carefully chosen professional development programs can address these problems. For example, an administrator who has been thrown into the development of an assessment program, without much background or time to research the field, may be able to construct the necessary framework by attending the annual meeting on assessment sponsored by the American Association for Higher Education. Although it may be difficult to identify entire programs that meet this goal, it can still be possible to identify a number of sessions at a convention that provide theoretical perspective on an issue or a related set of issues.

Enhancing a Personal Leadership Style. Most administrators develop a personal management and leadership style simply by doing their jobs.

But the pressures of daily job requirements afford little opportunity for an administrator to observe that style, to analyze the usefulness of its components, and to improve the style. It is necessary to step back to get some perspective and objectivity in order to really improve on one's own leadership style. Programs such as those sponsored by the National Institute for Leadership Development at Arizona State University are explicitly designed for this purpose. The goals of these programs (Leaders for Change, Leadership for a New Century, the Leaders' Project) are to help women administrators prepare for the next career step by strengthening their leadership styles and capacities. Such programs also provide the opportunity to consider leadership style not only in the context of a current job but also in the trajectory of preparing for the next career step.

On-Campus Opportunities

While some institutions have long recognized the benefits of providing their own on-campus development opportunities, the concept is only just beginning to spread. Initially, such activities are usually informal—a group of women in administrative positions get together once a month for a brown bag lunch to discuss common managerial problems, department chairs gather informally outside of the regular dean's meetings to share concerns and information, administrators involved in various facets of programming for freshmen meet irregularly to compare notes on the effects of their activities on students. The informal meetings and groupings that prove useful become formalized with mailing lists and assigned meeting rooms and times. Or a senior administrator, energized by a particular professional development experience, launches a similar activity on her campus. No matter the route, organized on-campus opportunities tend to grow from the grass-roots needs of each particular community, but in an entrepreneurial way those needs can be identified, articulated, and shaped by anyone who wants to take the initiative.

Most administrators are so busy with their own jobs that they rarely take a moment to look around at their institutions and creatively think about opportunities for their own development. There is slowly a growth in stories about two administrators who "swapped" jobs for a semester so each could learn another area or of an administrator who volunteered to take on a difficult project in return for free time later to pursue another project of personal interest. As these experiences become more prevalent, more administrators will think of similar openings on their own campuses.

Off-Campus Opportunities

Although there has long been a variety of professional development programs for administrators, few of these addressed the specific needs of people new to administration or promoted to new levels of jobs. Recently, a number of new programs have appeared that address these needs in particular. Associations are the primary providers of such programs, either in conjunction with their annual meetings or as freestanding seminars.

Of course, new administrators or those administrators new to a particular level of responsibility can also derive significant benefit from participation in general professional development programs. Such programs can be roughly categorized into four types: national institutes and internships, administrative conferences, conventions and annual meetings, and seminars, workshops, and meetings.

National Institutes. Considered by many to be the most prestigious of higher education professional development opportunities, these programs are intensive, two weeks in length or longer, sponsored by nationally known universities and higher education associations, and highly competitive, with comprehensive curricula exploring issues of education, management, and leadership. Participants are generally drawn nationally and even internationally, from the full range of types of institutions and the entire gamut of positions within the academy. Typically, an administrator participates only once in a national institute, although a small but growing number of administrators are benefiting from participation in a different program at each successive level of their careers. Examples include the Fellows Program (American Council on Education), the Institute for Educational Management and the Management Development Program (Harvard University), the College Management Program (Carnegie-Mellon University), Higher Education Resource Service (HERS) programs (Bryn Mawr and Wellesley colleges).

Administrative Conferences. Of shorter duration (several days to less than two weeks in length) than the national institutes, administrative conferences also focus on issues of education, management, and leadership. They are sponsored by a number of highly respected academic institutions and associations. Unlike the national institutes, which typically seek participants across a wide range of types of institutions and positions, administrative conferences usually focus on a particular segment of institutions or a specific type of position. Curricula are also comprehensive and often intensive, but programs are often designed to include time for reflection and significant interaction with the other participants in leisurely settings. Many administrative conferences are particularly suitable for new administrators or those new to a particular level of responsibility, whether through specific design of the program or through special activities for newcomers. Examples of administrative conferences include the National Conference of Academic Deans (Oklahoma State University), the Troutbeck Program for Presidents (Educational Leadership Project of the Christian A. Johnson Endeavor Foundation), Leadership Development Program (Center for Creative Leadership, Greensboro, North Carolina), and the Institute for the Management of Lifelong Education (Harvard University).

Conventions and Annual Meetings. All of the national higher education associations sponsor some sort of annual or biannual convention or meeting. These usually last from two to five days, are held in hotels in major cities, and focus on educational issues relevant to the members of the association. Sessions vary in format, including speeches, panel discussions, small group discussions, and workshops. The large numbers of participants at these events provide many benefits: the opportunity for interaction with many others, the volume needed to attract highly renowned speakers, and the diversity that engenders sessions on a wide range of topics. Different associations (and thus their annual meetings) are useful at different points in an administrative career. For example, a new graduate dean may become involved with the Council of Graduate Schools, then switch involvement to a sector association such as the American Association for State Colleges and Universities upon moving into a chief academic officer position in a state institution, and then add involvement in the American Council on Education upon starting a presidency.

Seminars, Workshops, and Meetings. Over the course of a career, the majority of professional development experiences of an administrator fall into this category, which includes short programs of one to three days that are sponsored by a wide variety of associations, institutions, foundations, government agencies, private companies, and consulting firms. Typically, these programs focus on specialized issues and problems in both the educational and management areas. Most programs for new administrators fall into this category.

Self-Created Activities. Increasingly, administrators are following the lead of faculty and creating their own professional development experiences. While the tradition is well established for faculty to create scholarly and professional experiences for sabbaticals and the resources needed to support such individually created activities are readily available, such opportunities are only just becoming available for administrators. Few institutions offer administrative sabbaticals, but an increasing number of administrators are stitching together their own experiences in creative ways. For example, a new dean of student affairs spent a day of each week of her first semester on the job visiting the chief student affairs officers of nearby institutions to learn about their programs and organizations.

Opportunities for New Administrators

Many associations and institutions now offer specific programs for new administrators. These programs have typically been developed with an emphasis on the difficulties of entering a new position as well as on the unique responsibilities and activities of the administrative newcomer. The following is a sampling of the range of programs available.

Presidents. Most of the national sector associations sponsor special introductory programs, either as freestanding seminars or as designated sessions within an annual meeting. For example, the American Association for Community and Junior Colleges and the American Association for State Colleges and Universities both offer summer seminars that include new and experienced presidents as a way to introduce new presidents to their jobs. Harvard University and the Institute for Educational Management now sponsor the Harvard Seminar for New Presidents, a five-day seminar to prepare new presidents for the multiple responsibilities and constituencies of their new jobs.

Academic Officers. Associations, often in conjunction with institutions, are also key providers of programs for administrators new to a particular level of academic responsibility. For example, a new assistant or associate dean can attend the Management Development Seminar for Assistant and Associate Deans sponsored by Academic Affairs Administrators and the University of Illinois. Many academic sector associations sponsor seminars to introduce new deans to the issues and networks of the field. Examples include the New Deans Seminar (American Assembly of Collegiate Schools of Business), the New Deans Institute (American Association of Colleges for Teacher Education), the Executive Development Seminar for Deans (Association of American Medical Colleges), the Seminar for New Deans (Council of Colleges of Arts and Sciences and American Conference of Academic Deans), and the Summer Workshop for Graduate Deans (Council of Graduate Schools). Typically, curricula focus on introducing new deans to the art and practice of college administration, budgeting, leadership style, curriculum and program development, human resource management, and fundraising. Institutional sector associations are the typical providers of programs for new academic vice-presidents. For example, the American Association for State Colleges and Universities annually organizes an Academic Leadership Institute to provide administrative skills and professional renewal for chief academic affairs officers.

Department Chairs. Many academic associations organize special meetings for department chairs at their annual meetings. For those associations without formal meetings, department chairs typically find ways to congregate to discuss their common problems and challenges. The most popular professional development program specifically designed for new department officers is the Department Leadership Program offered by the American Council on Education. The goal of the program is to improve administrative and leadership skills, to encourage dialogue on relevant issues, and to explore leadership issues. Sessions address faculty evaluation, faculty development, legal liability, decision making, change efforts, and performance counseling. This workshop can also be brought on-campus to address the professional development needs of the entire group of department chairs of an institution.

Other Administrative Positions. Other administrative officers can explore professional development at various career stages compliments of their supporting associations. For example, the National Association for Student Personnel Administrators, in conjunction with the American Council on Education, sponsors the annual Richard P. Stevens Institute for Student Personnel for deans and vice-presidents of student affairs. The National Association of College and University Business Officers (NACUBO), with sponsorship from Marriott Education Services, supports an annual Executive Leadership Institute to enhance existing leadership skills, expand self-knowledge, and exchange ideas regarding management. The regional NACUBO associations also sponsor management development institutes for college business officers. The Williamsburg Development Institute is principally designed for beginning professionals in areas of institutional advancement.

Planning for Professional Development

The value of professional development programs can be enhanced, both for the individual and the institution, through careful preparation and planned follow-through. Initially, an administrator should be aware of the types of programs attended by those in similar positions. What seems to be available? What is popular and why? What benefits seem to be derived from the experience? It is useful to collect information on programs, even if immediate participation is not feasible or desirable.

After identifying a program for participation, an administrator should do some research to understand the curriculum and organization. What is the style of pedagogy and does it meet one's preferred learning style? What other types of administrators typically attend? What types of follow-up does the program afford?

After registering for a program, it is useful for administrators to widely broadcast their participation and to discuss the goals, content, and format of the program with colleagues. Although there may be topics that are not immediately interesting or applicable to a participant, they may be of great interest to colleagues and the participant can then serve as their eyes and ears. Colleagues who have attended the program may have advice on ways to maximize the benefits and minimize the weaknesses of the program. For major programs and national institutes, which typically have unique formats and pedagogies, it is useful to contact past participants for inside information. What would the alumni have done differently to prepare for the experience? What advice would the alumni give on ways to derive the most value from the experience?

Before leaving for the program, the participant should consider how he or she is going to collect information and document the learning experience. What is the best way to take notes? What is the best way to gather materials? How does one get the materials home so that they can be useful back on the job?

Particularly at conventions, smart administrators plan ahead to meet colleagues and people with whom they want to be certain to have interactions. This could be as simple as checking that a colleague at another institution will be attending and making a lunch date, or as extensive as planning a meeting to gather administrators from other institutions to have a discussion on a particular topic not covered on the convention's agenda. It is not unusual to see conventioneers checking the roster of participants at the back of the program before reading the descriptions or program sessions at the front of the brochure.

After attending a program, it is helpful to report on the event—and what was learned and accomplished—to whomever sponsored one's participation. Distribute collected handouts and copies of notes from sessions to colleagues. Participants who give some thought to how to organize note-taking before a program will benefit at the end by spending less time in making materials and notes accessible to others.

Conclusion

Professional development programs provide a wealth of learning experiences to those administrators who think strategically about the usefulness of these activities to themselves and to their institutions. Few supervisors reach out to help the administrators in their charge to think creatively about participation in such programs. It is up to individuals to survey the range of programs and to find those that best match their needs, both for the present job and for career development.

Sharon A. McDade is an associate in Education and former director of the Institute for Educational Management, both at the Graduate School of Education, Harvard University.

Those who aspire to administrative positions in higher education need to understand both the advantages and the risks inherent to mentoring relationships.

Mentor Relationships: Those That Help and Those That Hinder

Linda K. Johnsrud

Lynn X., assistant dean of the College of Arts and Sciences (CAS), appreciated the time and support that the CAS dean Sam Y. had given her over the past three years. He had encouraged her to finish her doctoral dissertation and then recruited her for her current position. He continued to take an active interest in her career progress. Her recent assignment from him, the faculty-student summer research project, had provided her with valuable experience in initiating a new program as well as exposing her to numerous faculty and staff members across the campus. She had been hesitant to take it on but she was glad she had relied on his assessment of her ability. Although it was reassuring to know that Dean X. was there to defend her efforts (as he had last spring with the administrative handbook fiasco), she had gained confidence in her own judgment and her administrative skills. She felt good about her relationship with the dean. She knew he was readily available to provide counsel and support, but she also knew that he respected her abilities and enjoyed her increasing independence.

Steve A. had served as associate director of financial aid for three years. He had been steadily promoted from financial aid counselor to assistant director and then to associate, but he now felt stuck. His supervisor, Dr. William B., had been the director of financial aid for ten years and looked as if he would stay in the job until his retirement. Steve had always enjoyed working for Dr. B. and was loyal to his long-time boss. Dr. B. had taught him the ropes. From Steve's perspective, they were now a team, but he was slowly realizing that he was unknown within the university administration. Dr. B. had given him increasing responsibilities but they were within a narrow sphere. Steve had become a specialist despite his interest in broader roles within the administration. He felt as if he had learned as much as he could within his position, but he was not at all sure what direction he should next take in his career. He also knew that Dr. B. counted on him to run the office, a task for which he was well trained, but lately he wondered if he could succeed in any other arena. He hesitated to speak with Dr. B. about his career—he did not want him to feel that he was ungrateful for the years of support.

Despite the widespread and popular attention mentoring has received in the past decade, concerns have been increasingly voiced about the potential problems inherent to mentoring relationships. Much of the early work on mentoring in the organizational literature portrayed these relationships as vital to career development in organizations (Hennig and Jardim, 1977; Jennings, 1971; Kanter, 1977; Roche, 1979), and the higher education community was inclined to adopt similar thinking in relation to careers, both faculty and administrative, within the academy (Hall and Sandler, 1983; Moore, 1982; Rowe, 1981). Although mentors have come to be seen as the key to advancement within large organizations, the conflict and disappointment that can be experienced in a mentoring relationship have been acknowledged. Recently, however, some writers have criticized mentor relationships as hierarchical, dependent, and exploitive and have cautioned against entering such relationships (Haring-Hidore and Brooks, 1987; Swoboda and Millar, 1986).

Those who aspire to administrative positions in higher education need to understand both the advantages and the risks inherent to mentoring relationships. A mentor can be enormously helpful in building an administrative career in higher education. Nonetheless, careers have been built without mentors, and some mentoring relationships are debilitating. The purpose of this chapter is to offer a balanced perspective regarding the role of mentoring in administrative career development and to identify other supportive relationships in the workplace that can contribute to career success.

Mentoring Defined

Mentoring is relatively rare in its strictest definition. Moore and Salimbene (1981) define the mentoring relationship as an intense, lasting, and professionally centered relationship between two individuals in which the more experienced and powerful individual, the mentor, guides, advises, and assists in any number of ways the career of the less experienced, often younger, upwardly mobile protégé. Given this definition, it is not surprising that mentoring is not a common experience. The relationship requires a long-term reciprocal commitment of energy and time. It requires two people who come together at a mutually opportune time and who respect and enjoy one another enough to spend significant amounts of time together.

Although mentoring as defined here is rare, helpful relationships in the workplace are not. In a large national study of the role of mentoring in the careers of 1,888 upper-level administrators in higher education, respondents reported an average of five relationships that had a significant influence on their careers (Scollay, Tickamyer, Bokemeier, and Wood, 1988). Although they reported that these relationships had a mean duration of six to twelve years, they tended not to use the terms "mentor" or "protégé." Rather, respondents were more likely to select "supervisor" and "subordinate" as descriptors of relationships that they perceived had a significant, positive career influence.

The difficult in labeling relationships results from the ambiguity that surrounds the functions of mentoring. Patron, role model, sponsor, coach, and adviser are terms used to refer to persons who have provided some sort of career assistance. According to Kram (1985), the functions of the mentoring relationship are developmental and can be divided into career functions and psychosocial functions. The career functions she describes include sponsorship, coaching, provision of exposure and visibility, and challenging work assignments. These specific career-enhancing efforts are differentiated from functions that attend to the development of the whole person, such as acceptance and confirmation, counseling, role modeling, and friendship. Essentially, mentors enhance the position of the protégés by enabling the development of their skill and competence in a supportive environment. Much of what mentors do is testing and evaluating (Moore and Salimbene, 1981). By creating opportunities for protégés to expand their experience, take on new challenges, and test their limits, mentors propel their protégés forward (sometimes faster and further than protégés even find comfortable). At the same time, mentors provide the ongoing assessment and feedback that allows protégés to recognize their strengths and weaknesses and to develop their skills in rigorous, yet nurturing, environments.

Being taken "under the wing" of a mentor can be both a heady and humbling experience. The headiness is a result of being "chosen" to receive special attention, of being aware that an accomplished senior person sees potential that is worthy of his or her time to develop. The humility is a result of the recognition that there is much to learn, that embarrassing mistakes will be made, and that the guidance and protection of another can make the difference between success and failure. There is probably no other single relationship that can be as instrumental in enhancing an administrative career in higher education than a quality mentoring relationship.

Colleges and universities are complex professional organizations with ambiguous goals, idiosyncratic lines of communication, and highly specialized personnel. Navigating the administrative channels takes experience and savvy. Entry level and midlevel administrators often come into their positions well qualified to do their jobs. For example, fiscal specialists may have strong backgrounds in accounting or finance, student affairs staff members may bring significant experience in counseling or programming, and institutional advancement specialists may have developed their skills in the private sector. Despite their functional expertise, these administrators may not understand the contexts in which they work. Mentors provide the insight into the politics, the social norms, and the culture of the higher education organization that enables protégés to move forward.

As invaluable as quality mentoring can be, not all such relationships fulfill their potential. Some are simply more helpful than others; some are detrimental. It is vital for those building careers in higher education to recognize the characteristics of mentoring relationships that help versus those that hinder.

Characteristics of Mentoring Relationships That Help

The fictitious vignette describing the relationship between Lynn X. and Dean Y. underscores a relationship built on trust and communication. It is clear that Dean Y. took the time to become well acquainted with Lynn and that the two have communicated over several years regarding her career development. He gives her honest feedback about her strengths and weaknesses, and she trusts his assessment and encouragement. Dean Y. creates opportunities for Lynn to perform, and as a result she increases her skills as well as her confidence. Moreover, the opportunities result in the visibility and exposure that are critical to advancing within an organization. Lynn is given the opportunity to demonstrate her abilities, but Dean Y. provides a "safety net" for her protection. His sponsorship allows her to risk failure without paying a high price.

Dean Y. and Lynn are mutually interested in her career development. Both have much to gain from their relationship. Dean Y. enhances the productivity of his staff and cultivates talent for the institution. Lynn gains from his investment in her as she increases in competence and confidence. And most important for her long-term development is his encouragement of her independence. There is clearly a mutual respect between Lynn and Dean Y. He has shown a close and personal interest in her career progress but he has not become inappropriately involved in her life. He has maintained his role as supervisor and mentor. He has not allowed her to become dependent on him. He has reinforced her capacity for independent judgment. The relationship is one of integrity and maturity between two adults who share a common interest.

Characteristics of Relationships That Hinder

The fictitious vignette describing the relationship between Steve A. and Dr. B. presents a very different situation. Despite the amount of support Dr. B. has shown Steve through promotions and increased responsibilities, Steve now feels stymied. The most significant characteristic of the relationship may be his hesitance to discuss his concerns about his future with his mentor. Their lack of communication undermines the potential of the relationship. Both Steve and Dr. B. seem to have focused on the short-term progress of Steve's career. His promotions were necessary to his advancement within his administrative unit, but it appears that Steve and Dr. B. have different expectations for the long term. Although Steve's skills were enhanced and his career developed, he feels that he is now at a dead-end. It may be that Steve's expectations are not appropriate from Dr. B.'s perspective or that Dr. B. does not choose to cultivate talent that will leave his supervisory purview. Unfortunately, their mutual expectations were not discussed and clarified.

Although Steve's loyalty to his mentor is appropriate, in this case it is hampering his ability to discuss his own career needs. Steve does not trust Dr. B. to consider what is best for Steve's career development. Rather, he fears that he will be seen as "ungrateful," a reaction that suggests the emotional involvement between the two is not appropriate to the enhancement of Steve's career. Moreover, Steve has become dependent on working for Dr. B. in an area that Steve knows well. For this relationship to encourage Steve's growth, opportunities should be created that will broaden his skills as well as his confidence. He needs to gain a sense of his own independence. It is not clear in this vignette that Dr. B. is deliberately exploiting Steve, but he is the person who could provide the opportunities and the feedback to diminish Steve's dependency and promote his career growth.

Although this is a relationship that has been of help to Steve, it is clear that as a mentoring relationship, it falls short of its potential. At this stage of Steve's career, the relationship seems detrimental, but it is inappropriate to lay blame on either the mentor or the protégé. Both share responsibility for the quality of the relationship, and both need to work at clarifying and communicating their mutual expectations.

Cultivating Quality Mentoring Relationships

"When mentoring is good, it can be very, very good, but when it is bad, it is awful." Even the second fictitious vignette described here is not "awful." There are relationships, however, in which protégés are exploited: emotionally, sexually, and professionally. Inappropriate emotional ties have been forged, sexual harassment is all too common, and original work has been stolen. The importance of recognizing the potential for such exploitation is obvious, but, practically, it is not easy to anticipate situations that may prove to be unhealthy or negative. Beyond listening to the warnings of those who may have had prior experience with individuals, the best defense seems to be honest and up-front clarification of expectations by both mentor and protégé. Trust develops over time, and the degree of trust necessary for a quality mentoring relationship suggests that relationships should be entered with some caution and built over a significant period of time. Most mentoring relationships that are not helpful, however, are not awful; rather, they are awkward. The awkwardness has much to do with the headiness of the experience described earlier. The honor that is felt when one is singled out by an accomplished senior person makes it difficult to communicate dissatisfaction. The protégé often feels so grateful for the efforts of the mentor that it seems thankless to express any unmet wishes or hopes. Once again the importance of clarifying goals and expectations up-front needs to be stressed. A mentor and protégé need to acknowledge that they are, in fact, mentor and protégé; they need to talk about what that means to each of them, and they need to set the stage for ongoing conversations about their perceptions of the relationship. Neither can communicate alone; both share in the responsibility for openness and honesty.

Identifying Potential Mentors and Other Helpful Relationships

The difficult of finding a mentor is often expressed by entry and midlevel administrators. Some institutions have created formal programs to couple senior administrators with aspiring junior staff for career development. Although such programs are well intended and can be highly beneficial, mentoring relationships demand a personal connection that cannot be mandated. Programs can initiate contact between a potential mentor and protégé, but the quality of their relationship will depend on the personal rapport and trust they develop as they spend time together.

Schmidt and Wolfe (1980) list a number of considerations for identifying a potential mentor, such as shared personal interests and value orientation, professional achievement, and accessibility as a role model. They suggest, however, that the most important factor may be the willingness of the mentor to commit personal time and energy to the relationship. What is apparent about these considerations is that they are not accomplishments listed on a resumé; rather, they are shared attributes discovered as two individuals come to know and respect one another. Thus, it may be unwise to identify a potential mentor, call for an appointment, and merely ask if he or she would be willing to serve. Rather, the protégé who is seeking a mentor needs to find ways of establishing a relationship with a potential mentor over a period of time. Soliciting advice about a specific project or program, asking for critical feedback on some aspect of performance, or volunteering to work on a project with a potential mentor are all means to becoming professionally acquainted.

Another and more formal approach is to arrange for an administrative internship under the supervision of a potential mentor. Some institutions have formal programs designed especially for advancing women and minorities, but personal arrangements for an internship to enhance career skills constitute a viable strategy for any aspiring administrator. An internship requires advance planning to secure the support of the appropriate administrators as well as to ensure that current responsibilities are met. One strategy is to have two peers in an administrative unit agree to alternate release time for internships and to cover for one another. Once working as an intern, the aspiring administrator has the opportunity to build a relationship with a potential mentor in an administrative area of interest.

There is debate about the wisdom of entering a cross-sex mentoring relationship. The likelihood of romance being suspected or assumed by others is a factor to be considered. Nonetheless, the dearth of senior women administrators significantly handicaps junior women if they must avoid having men as mentors. Moreover, such an assumption compromises the integrity of men who are genuinely interested in enabling the advancement of women in their institutions. Once again, caution needs to be exercised as well as the most professional of conduct.

As mentioned earlier, many administrators name their supervisors as individuals who have provided significant career assistance. Supervisors are in a unique role to provide career help because they can be in close contact with their staff members; they are in a position to assess their staff members' strengths and weaknesses, to provide constructive feedback, and to create opportunities for skill development. One caution regarding supervisor-as-mentor relationships is the reaction of peers (Hennecke, 1983). There is a danger that other staff members under the same supervisor will perceive favoritism. Another issue is that experienced by Steve A. His supervisor seemed more interested in keeping him in his administrative unit than in encouraging his career development within the institution. This conflict is real for supervisors when the career growth of their staff members means they move out of their supervisory purview. Supervisors must sometimes choose between the quality and productivity of their staff as a whole and the career enhancement of individual staff members. The supervisor's prior track record in this regard may be the best indicator for someone in search of a mentor. If it appears that few staff members move beyond the administrative unit, that is a good sign that although the supervisor may be good at supervision, he or she may not be committed to enhancing the careers of staff members at the organizational level.

One of the advantages of supervisor-as-mentor relationships is that this pairing avoids one of the pitfalls experienced by protégés: conflicting advice from a mentor and a supervisor. Although this may be a difficult situation and call for tactful handling, it does leave the decision making precisely where it ought to be: in the hands of the protégé. Having more than one individual interested in enhancing the career of an aspiring administrator lessens dependence on any one person. In fact, increasing attention is being given to "multiple mentors" (Hall and Sandler, 1983) in order to avoid the dilemmas sometimes associated with the intensity of the mentor-protégé relationship.

There are a number of relationships in the workplace that can be career-enhancing. The assistance that can be provided by peers and colleagues deserves particular attention (Kram, 1985; Shapiro, Haseltine, and Rowe, 1978; Pancrazio and Gray, 1982). Peers can provide support and feedback for one another. Rather than the coaching or advising functions of the mentor, peers are more likely to share information about the organizational context and assist one another in choosing strategies that promote career success. Although peers may not have the power or position of more senior administrators, they can help one another with contacts and introductions as well as create opportunities for exposure and visibility. Moreover, peers have the advantage of their shared status. The difficulty of the hierarchical nature of the mentoring relationship is avoided, as well as the potential for exploitation. Moreover, the mutual sharing by peers is not likely to breed the dependence that can easily characterize mentor-protégé relationships.

Kram (1985) cautions that competition between peers on the same staff may be one potentially negative attribute of peer relationships. Peers outside of the same administrative unit can minimize this difficulty. Also, it is vital that peers serve as positive reinforcers of career success for one another, and not reinforce, for example, a lack of confidence or an aversion to taking risks. Peers have the advantage of being readily available, and they can provide invaluable emotional and career support for one another. Nonetheless, close peer relationships, like mentor relationships, must be chosen wisely and built on mutual trust and communication.

Responsibilities and Options of the Aspiring Administrator

Aspiring administrators can build relationships with others to enhance their careers, but there are responsibilities within those relationships. Mentors offer unique opportunities for development, but protégés must be willing to listen, to take the advice and the risks, and to put in the time and energy that is demanded by an intense developmental relationship. Mentors often "go out on the limb" for protégés, and it is important that protégés do everything they can to justify the faith their mentors have in them. Mentors do not expect perfection but they do expect genuine, whole-hearted effort. For mentoring relationships to be positive and career-enhancing, like the relationship between Lynn X. and Dean Y., both participants must give their best efforts to meeting each other's expectations.

When mentoring relationships are not positive, like the relationship between Steve A. and Dr. B., the protégé does have options. Steve could choose to risk a negative reaction from Dr. B. and be open about his desire to gain broader career experience. He might plan an alternative experience for himself, such as a job rotation or an internship in another administrative area, and ask Dr. B. for his support. On the other hand, he might decide that he has gained what he can from Dr. B.'s tutelage and turn to other sources of career support. He could seek peers or colleagues who could help him create strategies to advance his career. He could volunteer for institution-wide projects, programs, or task forces. He could approach senior-level administrators in areas of interest to him for advice. He has options he can exercise on his own behalf.

Whether the aspiring administrator is in a mentoring relationship or some other career-enhancing relationship, it is important to remember who is in control. No matter how helpful mentors, supervisors, or peers are, career decisions are not theirs to make. Administrators striving to build careers in higher education must set personal career goals and make choices that feel right for them. Career-enhancing relationships can be invaluable, but ultimately personal growth and development depend on individual attributes such as quality performance and personal integrity. These are the foundations on which solid careers are built.

References

Hall, R. M., and Sandler, B. R. *Academic Mentoring for Women Students and Faculty: A New Look at an Old Way to Get Ahead.* Washington, D.C.: Project on the Status and Education of Women, Association of American Colleges, 1983.

Haring-Hidore, M., and Brooks, L. "Mentoring in Academe: A Comparison of Protégés' and Mentors' Perceived Problems." Paper presented at the annual meeting of the American Educational Research Association, Washington, D.C., April 20-24, 1987.

Hennecke, M. J. "Mentors and Protégés: How to Build Relationships That Work." *Training,* 1983, *20,* 36-41.

Hennig, M., and Jardim, A. *The Managerial Women.* New York: Anchor, Doubleday, 1977.

Jennings, E. E. *Routes to the Executive Suite.* New York: McGraw-Hill, 1971.

Kanter, R. M. *Men and Women of the Corporation.* New York: Basic Books, 1977.

Kram, K. E. *Mentoring at Work.* Glenview, Ill.: Scott, Foresman, 1985.

Moore, K. M. "The Role of Mentors in Developing Leaders for Academe." *Educational Record,* 1982, *63,* 23-28.

Moore, K. M., and Salimbene, A. M. "The Dynamics of the Mentor-Protégé Relationship in Developing Women as Academic Leaders." *Journal of Educational Equity and Leadership,* 1981, *2,* 51-64.

Pancrazio, S. B., and Gray, R. G. "Networking for Professional Women: A Collegial Model." *Journal of NAWDAC,* 1982, *45,* 16-19.

Roche, G. R. "Much Ado About Mentors." *Harvard Business Review,* 1979, *57,* 14-28.

Rowe, M. P. "Go Find Yourself a Mentor." In J. Farley (ed.), *Sex Discrimination in Higher Education: Strategies for Equality.* Ithaca: New York State School of Industrial and Labor Relations, Cornell University, 1981.

Schmidt, J. A., and Wolfe, J. S. "The Mentor Partnership: Discovery of Professionalism." *NASPA Journal,* 1980, *17,* 45-51.

Scollay, S. J., Tickamyer, A. R., Bokemeier, J. L., and Wood, T. A. "'Mentoring/ Sponsorship' Relationships in Higher Education Administrative Careers: An Exploratory Investigation." Paper presented at the annual meeting of the American Education Research Association, New Orleans, April 5–9, 1988.

Shapiro, E. C., Haseltine, F. P., and Rowe, M. P. "Moving Up: Role Models, Mentors, and the 'Patron System.'" *Sloan Management Review, 19* (3), 51–58.

Swoboda, M. J., and Millar, S. B. "Networking-Mentoring: Career Strategy of Women in Academic Administration." *Journal of NAWDAC, 1986, 49,* 8–13.

Linda K. Johnsrud is assistant professor in the Department of Educational Administration at the University of Hawaii at Manoa, Honolulu.

Understanding the conventions and culture of the academic marketplace can help candidates navigate the system and overcome barriers presented by the unwritten code of career mobility.

The Rules of the Game: The Unwritten Code of Career Mobility

Marlene Ross, Madeleine F. Green

Few people begin their careers in the professoriate intending to become administrators. For the most part, academics "fall into" careers in administration. For some, a stint as a department chair or dean is in fact an interlude in a teaching career. For others, the first administrative position turns out to be the beginning of a new phase of their careers. As one chief academic officer put it, "When I became a department chair, I thought I'd try administration and see if I was any good at it. It turned out that I really enjoyed it and my colleagues told me I did a good job. The rest is history."

In the academic culture, developing a taste for administration is not necessarily something one claims proudly. According to the prevailing academic mythology, one is supposed to take an administrative job with great reluctance, sacrificing to "take one's turn in the barrel" but longing for the classroom and the library. Happily, there seems to be growing recognition that this myth is not helpful to either individuals or the institutions they serve. And, indeed, it is only logical that administrators, like other professionals, should want to hold the positions they do and see them as a way to make a positive contribution to their institutions. Approaching a position with reluctance, or, worse yet, dread, does not bode well for one's future success.

Let us assume then, that our readers are among those individuals who are considering administrative positions because they seek the challenge and the opportunity to enhance their own job satisfaction and to make a difference at their respective colleges or universities. They hear a great deal about what they can and cannot do, about how the system works. They have heard the conventional wisdom and are trying to sort out what is true

NEW DIRECTIONS FOR HIGHER EDUCATION, no. 72, Winter 1990 © Jossey-Bass Inc., Publishers

and what is myth. What are the rules of the game? Are the written rules that appear in search committee guidelines and advertisements in the *Chronicle of Higher Education* the same as the unwritten ones? Like many others contemplating a career move in higher education, they wonder how to sort out all of the available information on administrative positions.

How one gets into the administrative marketplace and how one moves about are subjects of much speculation and hallway discussion at national meetings. This chapter discusses the recognized but generally unstated "rules" of career mobility in academic administration in light of research on the career paths of presidents and American Council on Education (ACE) Fellows and years of anecdotal data. (The ACE Fellows Program, begun in 1965, identifies and prepares future leaders in higher education. It has helped nearly one thousand men and women gain the experience and perspective necessary to assume significant leadership roles in our colleges and universities.)

It is important to note that issues in career mobility for administrative managers and those for professional staff are often quite different. Preparation for and movement in positions in administrative and business affairs, advancement, and some areas of student affairs are often idiosyncratic and even less predictable than career paths in academic administration. Many administrative managers have much more on-the-job training than targeted preparation. For example, if a person were to plan to become a financial aid officer, registrar, or director of alumni programs, how would that individual proceed? In many cases, next steps are as unpredictable as points of entry. Where does a talented public relations or affirmative action officer go next? While career ladders in academic affairs are also unpredictable, there are discernible patterns and these are the focus of this chapter.

One assertion that is true across the board in higher education administration is that there is significant turnover. A recent survey revealed a 24 percent turnover rate in thirty-two administrative job categories at U.S. colleges and universities between 1987 and 1988. Seventeen percent of presidencies changed hands compared to 24 percent of the chief academic officers (Blum, 1989, p. A1). Although beyond the scope of this chapter, the causes of job turnover are varied and warrant study and analysis to increase our understanding of leadership issues in colleges and universities. But whatever the causes, the data indicate that there are significant numbers of openings each year, providing opportunities for job mobility.

What, then, does an individual need to know to get one of these jobs? What are the unwritten rules of the academic marketplace that he or she must understand in order to navigate the system? While rules may define the parameters of the system, they are also meant to be tested and broken. Understanding the conventions and culture of the academic marketplace can help candidates navigate the system and overcome barriers presented by the unwritten code of career mobility. It can also help search committees and hiring officials evaluate the prejudices and biases that narrow choices rather than expand the pool of potential talent. An academic marketplace that opens options for talented individuals and enables institutions to select from the widest possible pool is a healthy one. Unfortunately, higher education is not there yet.

Thus, the following list of "rules" is not meant to validate or endorse them but rather to make them visible and understandable so that as colleges and universities seek administrative talent, and individuals seek administrative positions, both sides can openly confront the hidden barriers that too often remain unexamined and unchallenged and drive the process in directions that are counterproductive for all.

Career Mobility

Rule 1. *Mobility across institutional types is very limited.* Academic administrators tend to move within the same family of institutions—private liberal arts colleges, community colleges, or urban universities. This phenomenon seems to be a result of the biases of search committees: "If you have not already lived in our kind of institution, you will not know what to do when you get here." Some candidates are successful in making the leap, but it is the rare committee that will take the "risk" that experience in one kind of institution is useful preparation for working in another type. Individuals who are successful in moving from one institutional type to another have often had some experience earlier in their careers in that other type of institution. Thus, a candidate for a position in a private liberal arts college who has spent the majority of her career in public institutions may have more credibility if she were an undergraduate in a liberal arts college, even though that may have been a long time ago.

Green (1988) reported that most career movement of presidents occurred within the same type of institution. Sixty-eight percent of all presidents were recruited from the same or similar type of institution. The likelihood of presidents continuing their careers in the same or similar type of institution was highest for chief executive officers of community colleges (82 percent held their previous positions in that sector) and doctorate-granting universities (76 percent held their previous positions in that sector). Presidents of comprehensive universities and baccalaureate colleges had slightly more varied backgrounds: 62 percent of the former group held their prior positions at the same or comparable institutions, as did 55 percent of the presidents of baccalaureate institutions.

Rule 2. *There is more internal mobility than meets the eye.* We tend to think that all positions are filled through national searches. Many positions are never advertised, and a healthy proportion of those that are advertised are filled by inside candidates. While this practice has the benefit of providing opportunities within one's own institution, it can also have the disadvantage of not bringing in "new blood." Thirty-two percent of presidents moved into their positions from within the same institution. And 40 percent of presidents of specialized institutions were most likely to be recruited internally.

A 1981 study found that 55 percent of all administrators were internal candidates (Moore, n.d.). Sixty-two percent of student affairs officers held a previous position at their current institution, compared with 59 percent of academic affairs administrators and 54 percent of administrative affairs officers.

Rule 3. *There is a pecking order in U.S. higher education that restricts "upward" mobility to more prestigious institutions.* Movement is limited not only by institutional type but also by institutional prestige. It is difficult to move from a nonselective institution to a selective one, from a non-Ivy to an Ivy, and from a comprehensive institution to a doctorate-granting university. The career paths of presidents typify the situation. Only 15 percent of new presidents of doctorate-granting universities came from comprehensive universities, compared to 76 percent from the same or another doctorate-granting institution (Green, 1988, p. 19). Moving up in the pecking order usually requires a lateral move, a strong academic and publications record, and preferably some association in the past with that class of institution.

Rule 4. *There is also a pecking order among disciplines that is a factor in career mobility.* Degrees in the traditional liberal arts are highly valued by prestigious institutions and by "upwardly mobile" institutions seeking to enhance their reputations and status. Some consider a background in education or professional fields to have less academic legitimacy than a background in the humanities or sciences. And, indeed, even the social sciences are suspect to some. Thus, individuals with degrees in education or counseling will have a hard time obtaining deanships in arts and sciences; deans of education, business, and technology will be disadvantaged in their quests for academic vice-presidencies or in moving to more prestigious institutions.

The hierarchy of fields is demonstrated by the credentials of presidents in the various sectors. It may seem surprising at first that 43 percent of presidents hold their highest degrees in education (Green, 1988, p. 13), including 22 percent of all presidents who hold the Ed.D. degree. When these figures are examined closely, however, they reveal that there are significant differences among institutional types. At doctorate-granting institutions, 7 percent of the presidents hold their highest degree in education, while 65 percent have degrees in biological/physical/natural sciences, social sciences, and humanities. At comprehensive colleges and universities, the comparable figures are 25 percent and 56 percent, respectively; at baccalaureate colleges, 33 percent and 44 percent, respectively; and at two-year colleges, 71 percent and 19 percent, respectively (Green, 1988, p. 14).

At doctorate-granting institutions, 81 percent hold the Ph.D. degree and 2 percent hold the Ed.D., compared to comprehensive universities and colleges where 73 percent hold the Ph.D. and 13 percent hold the Ed.D.; baccalaureate colleges where 65 percent hold the Ph.D. and 15 percent hold the Ed.D.; and two-year colleges where 40 percent hold the Ph.D. and 40 percent hold the Ed.D. (Green, 1988, p. 12).

Rule 5. *Routes to the highest positions are incremental but not always predictable.* Career paths in academic administration are less clear-cut than one might suppose. Moore (1983) found little advance planning by the individual or by the institution for a specific career path to lead to a college presidency. However, having faculty experience was found to be the main entry qualification for most top administrative posts (Moore, 1983), even among chief student affairs officers (Ostroth, 1984). Few people skip several rungs on the ladder. Seventeen percent of all presidents were recruited from other presidencies, while 42 percent were vice-presidents immediately prior to their presidencies (Green, 1988, p. 15). We might expect that most of the presidents who held vice-presidencies as their prior position were vice-presidents for academic affairs. In fact, only 23 percent of all presidents held this prior position. Forty-one percent of the presidents held other positions before assuming their presidencies: 19 percent were deans/directors, 8 percent were faculty/chairs, 2 percent came from the K–12 sector, 7 percent from outside academe, and 5 percent from other posts.

Although one might also expect an academic officer to start as a faculty member and then proceed from the position of department chair, to dean, and then to chief academic officer, Moore's (1983, p. 74) data indicate that no provosts followed that career path. Rather, 40 percent were department chairs before becoming provosts and 48 percent held faculty positions. No one became a provost without first serving as a faculty member, a chair, or a dean.

Credentials and Experience

Rule 6. *The credentials one needs to get the job are not necessarily the same ones needed to do the job.* It is no surprise that colleges and universities are even more credential conscious than the society at large. Thus, an institution aspiring to greater "excellence" may be tempted to look for a dean or president with impressive academic credentials, though the task at hand might really be raising money to fund good programs or building consensus among the faculty about needed academic reforms. The conventional wisdom holds that an academic leader must have credibility with faculty and other academic administrators. Such credibility is frequently related to a candidate's association with prestigious institutions or success as a scholar. While academic accomplishments do provide credibility and can help an administrator in his or her capacity of role model, they provide no assurance that he or she is qualified to actually do the job of dean, chief academic officer, or president.

Moore's (1983) research shows that achieving the rank of full professor is an important prerequisite for administrators: 91 percent of the presidents holding academic rank were full professors, as were 90 percent of the provosts and 80 percent of the academic deans.

Rule 7. *Institutions tend to hire administrators who reflect the image of what they would like to be rather than what they are.* A review of advertisements in the *Chronicle of Higher Education* reveals requests for qualifications that many incumbents could not meet. Yet the committees that establish criteria often believe that this is the way to change their institution into what they would like it to be. Unfortunately, institutions seeking to improve often look to a single model of excellence. That model values research over teaching, becoming more selective rather than serving students more effectively. These institutions seek to attract individuals to administrative positions who can help them achieve these aspirations, whether through their past association with more prestigious institutions or through the "excellence" of their academic records as viewed through the conventional measure of research productivity. While seeking out such individuals is not inherently harmful and may sometimes be beneficial, it is unwise to expect that an individual who embodies the qualities the institution desires can have the desired positive effect without many other factors in place.

Rule 8. *People with nontraditional credentials often get their first break in a staff position, circumventing the search process.* Search committees often are inflexible, following the conventional rules of the game. Individuals who want to switch areas, for example, from academic affairs to governmental relations or from student affairs to academic affairs, have a hard time getting their first positions because they do not have the experience or the credentials. Search committees will almost always put resumés that do not demonstrate closely related experiences in the "no" pile. Similarly, people with credentials in less desirable fields will have difficulty getting through the conventional criteria that govern the sorting process of search committees. Thus, a staff position (assistant, associate, or assistant to) that does not depend on a search committee may provide the needed first opportunity for these individuals. Once an individual has served successfully as an assistant vice-president for academic affairs or as an associate dean, the next step is easier. Thus, while the conventional wisdom holds that "assistant to" or assistant/associate positions are likely to be dead-ends, this is not necessarily the case. For some people, these positions are invaluable training grounds and stepping-stones.

The Search Process

Rule 9. *At the beginning of a search, the unstated qualifications for the position reflect a collective wish for change, no matter how effective the incum-*

bent was. A new dean or provost brings the promise of change for the better, even if the previous person was successful. Somehow there is a felt need to compensate, to recruit for those qualities that were weak in the incumbent. Rejection for a position may mean nothing more than that the individual is too similar to the person who previously held the position. As one unsuccessful candidate noted, "As soon as I found out that Dean X. was a biologist, I knew I was dead in the water. I could tell that the search committee thought that I couldn't possibly bring a different perspective to the job because I was a biologist, too."

Rule 10. *The title one sees is not always what one gets.* There is general agreement that the title "president" or "chancellor" refers to the chief executive officer. But beyond that, there is little consensus among campuses. "Assistant to the president" can be a secretarial position or a high-level professional with line responsibility for certain operational areas. A dean may have three hundred faculty in his or her college, or direct a very small program. Some variations in job responsibility will vary with institutional type and size; others are simply idiosyncratic to that institution. The only way to understand these differences is to review carefully the institution's organizational chart and request clarification regarding the position's responsibilities.

Rule 11. *If an individual decides to enter a search, it is preferable to be nominated rather than to apply for the job.* Here the mythology comes into play that it is better to be sought after than to volunteer. While it is common knowledge that there is usually little difference between an application and a nomination, rules of the game dictate that it is better to be nominated than to apply. Of course, an individual would be unwise to simply sit back and hope that a friend or colleague will think to take the initiative to nominate him or her (though it does sometimes happen). Seeking a nomination is a simple matter; it requires asking a friend, colleague, mentor, or supervisor to write a letter on one's behalf. This means supplying the nominators with useful, up-to-date information about one's qualifications and letting them know about the kinds of positions of interest. The common practice is to ask for a nomination for a specific job when it is advertised.

A frequent question is whether it is desirable to be nominated by a person of high position and significant prestige. More important than the position or prestige of the nominator is the ability of that individual to speak credibly about the candidate and the respect he or she would command in the institution conducting the search. According to the conventional wisdom, a president of an elite liberal arts institution has more prestige than a dean of a community college, but the former has far less credibility as an advocate of a candidate's ability to lead in a two-year institution. Also, a strong nomination means that the nominator knows the candidate well and can speak with conviction about his or her accomplishments and attributes. A letter revealing that the nominator does not really know what the candidate can do is far less helpful than one that is an authentic and enthusiastic endorsement.

Rule 12. *Higher education is a surprisingly small world.* Word gets around about individuals with multiple applications. It is important to think judiciously about one's actual interest in a position. One should never request a nomination just to test one's viability as a candidate, where the plan is to turn down the position if offered. Between the active national grapevine in higher education and the information that flows freely in states governed by sunshine laws, there are very few secrets. Thus, people tend to know who has been in many searches, who has turned down a number of positions, and who has consistently been a "bridesmaid."

Rule 13. *Very few people actually know if a search is "wired" and it is usually difficult to find out.* As we have noted above, many positions are filled internally. Some of these positions are never advertised, but others are, and the internal candidate is selected from a national pool. This may happen for several reasons. First, internal candidates are known quantities, and when compared with the prospect of taking a risk on an unknown individual, the hiring official may decide it is better to go with a proven success than an uncertain future. In this instance, the search is not wired, but rather the insider has the advantage. In other cases, however, being known can just as easily work against the insider. The search committee may strongly feel the need for change and believe that an unknown person has more potential to reveal than the insider, whose faults and limitations are already clear. In either case, it is impossible to know as an outsider whether or not there is an inside candidate and whether he or she is the likely choice. Only a source on the search committee willing to share that uncomfortable truth can provide insight into that question.

Sometimes a position will be targeted for a woman or minority (but not necessarily a specific individual). A committee may be quite explicit about this preference, or affirmative action may figure in the committee's deliberations more than in their conversations with candidates.

Rule 14. *While women and minorities are now getting on the short lists more often, that does not mean they will automatically get the jobs.* Many institutions are making a good faith effort to recruit women and minority individuals to administrative positions. Some institutions require each short list to include women and minorities. But there is a long way to go from the short list to the chosen candidate, and many institutions are unable or unwilling to take the plunge and hire someone as different from them as a woman or a minority. Sometimes, the short list game is cynically played, and an institution may have no real commitment to diversity. For whatever reason, many majority women and minority men and women end up as "bridesmaids," on the short lists but not selected, especially in presidential searches. The glass ceiling still exists. The fallout of this phenomenon is candidates who are bitter and cynical about the search process.

It is worth noting, though we are now getting into politically charged and complex territory, that there is also fallout from the perception by white men that they are not viable candidates for positions because women and minorities are now getting preferential treatment. The underrepresentation of women and minorities in higher-level administrative positions suggests that such resentment derives more from the fear of what might be than from what actually is. The data corroborate this. Sagaria and Johnsrud (1987) reported that white men were overrepresented at the high administrative levels, while white women and minorities were overrepresented at the low administrative levels. In 1986, minority individuals represented 11.5 percent of administrators. African-Americans comprised 7.6 percent of administrators (including African-American administrators at historically black institutions); Hispanics, 2 percent; Asians, 1.5 percent; and American Indians, .4 percent (Green, 1989).

Green (1988, pp. 4–5) reported that 93 percent of college presidents are white. Minority individuals represent 7 percent of the presidents, with only 2 percent of predominantly white institutions headed by African-Americans. Women comprise 10 percent of the chief executive officers, with women and minorities underrepresented in doctorate-granting institutions. While some progress may have been made in the past five years, the majority of women and minority administrators are still in lower-level positions, slots traditionally occupied by women (librarians, deans of nursing or home economics) or minorities (heads of bilingual programs, affirmative action), and in institutions with high concentrations of women, African-Americans, or other minority groups.

Rule 15. *Because quality is in the eye of the beholder, the outcomes of searches are unpredictable and sometimes illogical.* Discussions of hiring, searches, and diversity inevitably involve assumptions about quality and excellence. The concept of quality is subject to many definitions that depend on individual biases as well as on institutional contexts and value systems. Thus, a search may proceed without the committee coming to grips with the meaning of quality in the context of a particular position. What makes a candidate inherently "qualified," or more or less qualified than others, is not self-evident; these are important discussions that often do not take place. Thus, the selection of the top persons from the candidate pool may not necessarily reflect a clear understanding of the meaning of quality in the context of that search. At best, the selection criteria may represent a common understanding of quality that is realistic for that particular institution and that expands the range of viable candidates rather than diminishes it. At worst, the choice of finalists may represent nothing more than political compromise, collective fatigue, or some vague wish about what quality might be at that institution.

Suggestions for Potential Candidates

Now that some of the rules of the game have been explicated, here are some useful career strategies to help potential candidates navigate the process of job seeking:

1. When considering a new position, learn as much as possible about the culture of the institution and the leadership styles of the leaders. Interview the institution while you are being interviewed. Be sure the institution is a place in which you will feel comfortable and be productive. Use your network of faculty and administrative colleagues to find out everything the search committee and hiring officials fail to tell you. Do not forget that the institution is wooing you and may tend to put on a good face whenever possible. You will need to work hard to find out the whole truth.

2. If you decide to pursue the position and ask for letters of recommendation, provide your nominator and referees with a description of the position as well as a few paragraphs updating your activities. Give them plenty of lead time before the letter is due, and be sure to let them know if the outcome is positive. If someone has been writing a number of letters on your behalf, it is only courteous to let that individual know personally that his or her efforts have paid off for you and that you have selected a particular position.

3. If you are selected, negotiate what you will need to get the job done. Negotiation after you have accepted the position or started it is much more difficult. If you are not selected, ask for feedback after a search. Turn a disappointment into a learning experience.

4. Our final suggestion is arguably the most important one, deriving from everything we have said above: Never take rejection personally. Remember that the academic marketplace is governed by a series of unpredictable and irrational forces. Thus, whether or not you get a job generally has little to do with whether or not you are qualified for it. Rather, your career mobility will depend on a series of factors, many of which you cannot control. As long as you remember that what may appear to be a linear and rational process is not that at all, you will be less likely to personalize your failures or to take your success in obtaining a job too seriously. Remember, you may have gotten the job not because you are intrinsically meritorious or right for the position but because you are not a biologist, or because someone really liked your style, or because you were in the right place at the right time. Your successes as well as your defeats may have nothing at all to do with your abilities.

References

Blum, D. E. "24-Pct. Turnover Rate Found for Administrators; Some Officials Are Surprised by Survey Results." *Chronicle of Higher Education*, Mar. 29, 1989, pp. A1, A14.

Green, M. F. *The American College President: A Contemporary Profile*. Washington, D.C.: American Council on Education, 1988.

Green, M. F. *Minorities on Campus: A Handbook for Enhancing Diversity*. Washington, D.C.: American Council on Education, 1989.

Moore, K. M. *The Top-Line: A Report on Presidents', Provosts', and Deans' Careers*.

University Park: Center for the Study of Higher Education, The Pennsylvania State University, 1983.

Moore, K. M. "A Quiz About Administrators' Careers." In *Leaders in Transition: A National Study of Higher Education Administrators*. University Park: Center for the Study of Higher Education, The Pennsylvania State University, n.d.

Ostroth, D. D. "Career Patterns of Chief Student Affairs Officers." *Journal of College Student Personnel*, 1984, 25 (5), 443-448.

Sagaria, M.A.D., and Johnsrud, L. K. "Administrative Intrainstitutional Mobility: The Structuring of Opportunity." Paper presented at the annual meeting of the Association for the Study of Higher Education, San Diego, California, February 13-17, 1987.

Marlene Ross is acting director of the Center for Leadership Development and acting director of the Fellows Program of the American Council on Education, Washington, D.C.

Madeleine F. Green is acting president of Mount Vernon College, on leave from her job as vice-president and director of the Center for Leadership Development at the American Council on Education, Washington, D.C.

While administrators at every level experience at least some role conflict and role ambiguity while they acclimate to their new jobs, if the dissonance is left unresolved, it can lead to lower job satisfaction and self-confidence, higher job tension and psychological strain, and greater feelings of futility and anxiety.

Bridging the Gap Between Expectations and Realities

Marilyn J. Amey

No matter how carefully we prepare for administrative job interviews, no matter how thoroughly we question those employed at the institutions, no matter how competent we feel to assume the responsibilities of new jobs, it seems inevitable that once the newness begins to wear off (and sometimes even sooner), we realize that our expectations of the jobs do not match the realities. What are the causes or sources of this gap between expectations and realities on the new job? Are there strategies we can use to bridge the gap? Though the nature of each administrative position and the substance of the gap itself are highly dependent on each individual organization, some elements of the gap between expectations and realities of a new job are consistent across college and university administrations. Fortunately, there are strategies that can help bridge the gap as administrators acclimate to new positions.

Elements of the Gap Between Expectations and Realities

While the list could be extended, five elements in particular are cited frequently in the literature as sources of dissonance for new administrators. These are role conflict or ambiguity, lack of systematic evaluation and feedback, scope of responsibilities and tasks, opportunities (or lack thereof), and academic or experiential preparation.

Role Conflict or Ambiguity. Administrators are often torn by conflicting job demands, differences of opinion with supervisors, and obligatory tasks they do not want to do or are very uncomfortable doing, such as terminating another person's employment. The dissonance caused by these

NEW DIRECTIONS FOR HIGHER EDUCATION, no. 72, Winter 1990 ©Jossey-Bass Inc., Publishers aspects of role conflict is not only common but sometimes overwhelming when an administrator is new to the job and lacks the means by which to resolve the conflicts. Another slightly different factor that contributes to the gap between expectation and reality is role ambiguity or uncertainty about the scope and responsibilities of the job, its objectives, and colleague expectations (Rasch, Hutchison, and Tollefson, 1986). While on paper a position may look fairly straightforward and clearly defined, the college or university administrator needs to recognize that many of the daily responsibilities and tasks fall under the "other" category of the job description. Colleague perceptions and expectations of the position may also significantly shape the way it can be enacted. Unfortunately, these may not be clearly conveyed until after an administrator has gotten into the job and becomes acquainted with the different personalities with whom he or she will interact.

Midlevel administrators seem to be the quintessential sufferers of role conflict and role ambiguity. They are the organizational "linking pins" (Scott, 1978) between the often-competing agendas and perceptions of vertical and horizontal constituents. Midlevel managers implement policy but seldom develop it; they provide service to others while also having control of others and their actions. They are simultaneously servants (support staff) and police officers (monitors of procedures). The scope of responsibilities for midlevel administrators can quickly become overwhelming, with increasing numbers of directives coming from above and demands from below. It takes time to gain a clear sense of how to prioritize tasks and reconcile conflicting agendas, as well as to whom and when one can say no, all of which are important in bridging the gap between expectations about the job and its realities.

Similar dissonance exists for academic deans who feel caught "in between": not quite a professor and not quite a senior administrator. Deans feel they sit "at the messy crossroads of education's snowy ideals and muddy politics," and that everyone wants "a piece" of them (Walterscheid, 1990, p. 2). Deans often find that their faculty colleagues see them in a different, and not always positive, light as they assume their new, administrative roles, especially when they were promoted from within their institutions. There is culture shock for everyone involved.

Likewise, academic vice-presidents and provosts find themselves trying to carve out a niche between the competing and often conflicting expectations and agendas of college presidents and faculty senates. The provost is torn between being the number-one staff member for the president and the faculty, on the one hand, and the number-two leader of the institution, on the other (Amey, 1989). If the president casts a long shadow, positively or negatively, it may be very difficult for others to clearly identify the roles, responsibilities, and individuality of an academic vice-president. Conversely, in colleges with very strong faculty senates, the authority and influence of the provost may be limited to staff status, as he or she is expected to serve at the pleasure of the faculty committee structure rather than act independently as the chief academic officer. Needless to say, role conflict and ambiguity are heightened for provosts when both scenarios are in effect simultaneously. Although administrators at every level experience at least some role conflict and role ambiguity while they acclimate to their new jobs, if the dissonance is left unresolved, it can lead to lower job satisfaction and self-confidence, higher job tension and psychological strain, and greater feelings of futility and anxiety.

Lack of Systematic Evaluation and Feedback. For administrators addressing that element of the gap between expectations and realities that is a function of role conflict, the early stage of socialization in their new jobs is the most likely time for role conflict to be dissipated or heightened (Louis, 1980). During this period, the expectations held by an administrator prior to assuming the position are tested against the realities of the work environment. The bigger the gap between these expectations and realities, the greater the sense of administrator dissonance, which usually leads to turnover if not resolved. One of the most important factors in mitigating this gap is the feedback one receives, both positive and negative. Yet, higher education organizations are notoriously negligent in providing timely, systematic, and useful feedback to administrators, and a total absence of training is common during the socialization period. Newcomers know when they have done something wrong, but they may be forced to learn as much by trial and error as by any systematic process of feedback and evaluation. New administrators who are unsure of the appropriate questions to ask or are afraid of appearing too insecure may be particularly reluctant to actively seek feedback early in the socialization period, thereby heightening the stress and dissonance of transition.

As in any organization, higher education administrators have multiple and diffuse responsibilities. Supervisors regularly add to these responsibilities other tasks that are not included in any written job description. Accurate identification of those aspects of the job in need of evaluation then becomes problematic. The reactive nature of many administrative positions may also mitigate against the use of heavily goal-oriented evaluations or assessments, such as those often found in the private sector (Kuh, 1983). Without a clear sense of how, when, and on what basis their performance will be evaluated, and without any systematic evaluation procedures, it is not surprising that administrators choose to look off campus to friends and peers for the kind of feedback, training, guidance, recognition, colleagueship, and rewards lacking within their own organizations. While this outward orientation may be a valuable strategy in bridging the gap related to performance evaluation and feedback, too much distancing from the organization can have its own negative side effects.

Scope of Responsibilities and Tasks. Moving up the administrative hierarchy can certainly provide new opportunities, challenges, and relationships. Yet, the move also seems to leave little time, if any, for those activities enjoyed at an earlier time. This gap between expectations and realities can sometimes feel like too great a price to pay for the challenges and benefits of administrative work. For instance, advancement for midlevel administrators in the student affairs area often means little time for working with students and developing ongoing relationships. In many cases, these student interactions were a primary incentive for initially choosing an administrative career. In academic administration, advancement means little time for teaching and even less time for research. Teaching almost becomes an escape for academic administrators. Their days are consumed by paperwork, problem solving, and meetings with other administrators. In describing the paperwork, one administrator said, "There's so much mundane but necessary nonsense attached to [the paperwork]. . . . It doesn't help me accomplish my immediate job or workload. . . . The stuff . . . never seems to go away" (Walterscheid, 1990, p. 4).

In general, administrators find their jobs come with far too much responsibility and too little authority, too few resources (human and fiscal) to accomplish what needs to be done, too much paperwork and red tape, and not enough time! Administrators have an in-box but can seldom find the out-box. The discovery that others have unrealistic expectations of how quickly things can be handled defines some of the day-to-day workload anxiety of many administrators. Rasch, Hutchison, and Tollefson (1986) found that the long hours required, or expected, filled with too many interruptions, were a considerable source of job tension and dissatisfaction for administrators at research universities. Certainly, the same argument could be made for those at other types of colleges and universities.

Opportunities or Lack Thereof. In most circumstances, people accept new positions that they believe will provide opportunities for personal and professional growth and development. However, problems arise when there is a gap between the opportunities thought to be available through the position and the realities found once in the job. A vertical move upward has come to imply greater latitude for decision making, more power and authority, and increased opportunity to make an impact—to create change—almost without consideration for the context in which the move is made. The realities are that many directors, department heads, deans, and vice-presidents may be far more constrained by the college or university's structure, norms, and values and by the responsibilities of others than is at first apparent. As evidence, one academic vice-president reports, "You have the responsibility without the authority" (Amey, 1989, p. 117). Reality, it seems, is a function of where in the hierarchy one is sitting!

Middle managers, the next role for entry-level administrators, have long been considered persons with limited opportunities and many restrictions, in part because of their coordinating function within the college or university. While those moving into positions of middle management may perceive an increase in status, middle managers actually have infrequent contact with faculty and senior administrators and are insulated by bureaucratic layers from the key decision makers of the institution. Austin and Gamson (1983) found that when interacting with faculty for the first time, many middle managers are even surprised at the limited professional respect they are afforded.

A similar lack of opportunity often awaits academic vice-presidents, a highly sought position for many administrator aspirants. Organizationally, academic vice-presidents are required to facilitate and advocate the agendas and issues of others, primarily the president and faculty. Doing so without becoming a slave to another's priorities or without becoming too duplicitous are dilemmas that ultimately affect an academic vice-president's opportunities for leadership and change (Amey, 1989).

Another gap in upper-level management opportunities stems from the fact that while an administrator may have acquired greater latitude in the new job to make decisions and set a course of action, it is now equally important to take a back seat and promote the work, efforts, and decisions of others. As one dean reports, "[You] have to learn to like standing backstage, to be unselfish and to let others shine" (Walterscheid, 1990, p. 4). The focus of an administrator's efforts also changes the higher in the organization he or she goes. At a point where an administrator may be particularly interested in affecting change, he or she is further removed from hands-on interactions and relegated the tasks of policy-making and paper processing. Upper-level administrators are responsible for seeing the "big picture" and subsequently setting appropriate policies that mid- and lower-level administrators will carry out, not for doing much of the implementation themselves. Again, rather than necessarily being able to do more, an upper-level administrator must rely on others to enact visions, agendas, and goals.

Finally, not every position that appears to provide greater opportunities (because it has done so in the past) may actually do so in the present. Opportunity is in large part determined by the person in the next upward position on the ladder. For instance, a supervisor may be unwilling to delegate important responsibilities or to share "plum assignments," thereby effectively limiting opportunities for growth, development, and institutional exposure of other administrators in the department. In another sense, the longer directors of units remain in their positions, the fewer upwardly mobile opportunities there are for assistant and associate directors. This is not to say that horizontal or upward vertical movement inherently provides no opportunity for growth and development. Opportunity still breeds more opportunity, just not for as many administrators as expect it (Kanter, 1977). Administrators need to be aware of the gap between expectations and realities caused by the organizational hierarchy and its effect on how they perceive themselves and their mobility and opportunities.

Academic or Experiential Preparation. Kanter (1977) describes another dimension of the gap when she speaks of administrators who become stuck because they have moved into jobs via the "wrong" paths and thereby lack sufficient and proper academic or experiential training to move beyond their present positions. In today's educational environments, the skills needed for senior administrative leadership cannot always be acquired through the line of traditional academic ascendancy (Krinsky, 1986). Search committees need to broaden the definition of the "right" path and look beyond traditional academic credentials when evaluating administrative candidates. This is particularly true in public-sector institutions where the ability to relate to elected officials has become critical. Today's administrators, at least at the level of deans and directors and above, need to be effective fund-raisers, to understand and be able to conduct broad institutional/college/unit planning and budgeting, and to be sensitive to labor relations, labor market issues, and human resource development. These skills are not likely to be formally taught in academic degree programs. Rather, they are gained through a wide variety of experiences, which need to be viewed as relevant credentials for prospective administrators.

Today's colleges and universities need administrative generalists, even though these institutions continue to develop and encourage specialists. This is particularly true for administrators who move from academic disciplines, which value specialization, into department chair or dean positions. The skills of a good teacher or researcher are not necessarily transferable to administrative jobs, where the abilities of delegating responsibilities, letting others take the spotlight, detaching one's emotions from explosive issues, motivating colleagues, managing crises, and solving problems are necessities. Unfortunately, "[a] great teacher may be a real bust as an administrator" (Walterscheid, 1990, p. 4) and may subsequently find the job filled with gaps between expectations and realities as he or she tries to adjust to new norms, skills, and behaviors. The analogy of the specialist assuming a generalist position can just as easily be drawn for those administrators who spend their careers advancing through one area of the institution and are looking to cross over into another unit or a more central administrative role. Although the required skills of the new job may look similar on paper, the context, level, and focus of decision making and the ability to understand the larger institutional environment may cause significant dissonance for the newly promoted administrator.

While the specialist/generalist issue is one side of the preparation argument, another side is the growing importance of academic credentials as criteria in upward mobility without a corresponding value ascribed to years of experience. As this imbalance is a fairly recent phenomenon (Moore, 1984), the valuing of a terminal degree over years of experience and local knowledge may come as a surprise to many long-time administrators. Loyal heads of units such as physical plant, business affairs, and student affairs who have built institutional careers are very susceptible to the predicament of reduced mobility due to lack of advanced degrees. While academic (teaching) experience might still be preferred in applicants for senior administrative posts in many areas of an institution, the credibility associated with a doctorate seems *essential* for a growing number of new hires or promotions throughout the university.

From an experiential perspective, the human resource element—the rallying of persons to work with and for a particular plan, decision, or program—may be the most critical to managerial success. Unfortunately, it is often also the element for which a new administrator is least prepared. The higher in the organization an individual moves, the more aware he or she becomes that administration is not a one-person operation. As one dean suggests, you have to be "a Tom Sawyer—you've got to get a bunch of people whitewashing the same fence" (Walterscheid, 1990, p. 4). And as a provost notes, "If you don't have the faculty with you, you're standing by yourself" (Amey, 1989, p. 83). Newly promoted administrators have to learn quickly that change will come less often from mandates and top-down decision making than from working with others. It is important to learn how the organizational system operates and to work within and through it.

In addition to all of the above issues, women administrators face other factors that curtail opportunities and widen the gap between expectations and realities. Tokenism (Kanter, 1977), accumulative disadvantage (Clark and Corcoran, 1986), and the old boys' network are only a few examples of behaviors and attitudes that can limit opportunities for women once they have accepted new administrative positions. Optimists speak of continuing progress for women administrators in colleges and universities, but realists recognize the continuing existence of a glass ceiling for women, which bars them from senior administrative positions, including presidencies, in most institutions (Morrison, White, and Van Velsor, 1987). Kathryn Moore (Chapter Nine) discusses many of these issues in the present volume.

Strategies for Bridging the Gap

There are several strategies available to new administrators for bridging the gap between expectations and realities.

Defining the Organizational Culture. Perhaps one of the most important and often-overlooked strategies is to understand the organizational culture and the different levels on which it exists. Within each college or university, there are at least three levels of culture of which administrators need to be aware: the culture of the college or university itself, the culture of the administrative profession at large, and the culture of the departmental unit (Clark, 1980). Different cultures respond to different leadership behaviors and management strategies; therefore, understanding the dynamics of these cultural levels can help reduce the dissonance that results from the gap between expectations and realities. Familiarity with the values, norms, rituals, and myths of an institution enables an administrator to recognize those behaviors and strategies most likely to reduce dissonance. An understanding of the culture provides administrators with a vehicle not only for assessing their respective institutions and departments but also for identifying tasks and appropriate roles for themselves, thereby reducing some of the dissonance caused by role conflict and role ambiguity. While not proposed as a panacea for bridging the gap, sense making, awareness of ideologies, rituals, symbols, and so on that motivate or alienate colleagues, and development of leadership skills are important components in administrative effectiveness.

Establishing Confidants and Communication Networks. Little research has been done on how new administrators choose their confidants and institutional informants, yet it is clear that these decisions can be critical to administrators' socialization and even to their success. Confidants can be instrumental in helping a new administrator become familiar with his or her unit and the organizational culture in general. They can serve as the foundation of initial communication networks, and if accurately tuned in to the organization, confidants can help a new administrator come to understand the difference between gossip and "organizational intelligence." Communicating effectively and being able to gather pertinent, accurate information for informed decisions are critical to an administrator's success. These skills can also play a role in how soon some aspects of the gap are resolved, or at least mitigated, such as rallying others' support, delegating responsibilities, addressing competing agendas, and actively seeking performance evaluation and feedback.

Understanding the Professional Anchoring of the Position. Not every administrative position is designed to have the same opportunities or future potential. Comparatively, some jobs are perceived as "fast-trackers," while others, such as "assistant to" positions, are often seen as dead-ends or limited in growth options. It is important to look closely at the professional anchoring of a position in order to accurately assess the opportunities and potential that may or may not exist.

In this discussion, professional anchoring refers to the predominant orientation and interaction patterns of a position. Some positions have an interdependent, outward focus where relationships and interactions with others inside and outside the unit are necessary to job performance. Those who work in academic advising, for instance, understand the importance of building relationships with faculty departments as well as with admissions and student orientation staffs in order to be effective. The outward focus keeps the administrator more aware of the larger college or university, its culture, and its means of functioning because attention is not primarily directed toward the unit. An alternate form of professional anchoring takes a more inward orientation, focusing on the unit itself and being less dependent on other areas outside the unit for daily job performance. This latter type of administrative position tends to be fairly self-contained and emphasizes more depth than breadth in professional growth. Administrators in "service units" of a college or university, such as housing and physical plant, are particularly likely to be in jobs that are inwardly focused, constricting their mobility by virtue of their increasing specialization and lack of larger institutional knowledge.

While it may not be within the purview of each administrator to always choose a more outwardly focused job, it is important to recognize the implications of professional anchoring for bridging some aspects of the gap between expectations and realities. Creative approaches to lateral growth, such as job expansion or extension, committee work, and special projects, can be viable alternatives for those who find themselves in positions that appear to have limited opportunities for professional development and upward mobility.

Conclusion

Strategies for bridging the gap between expectations and realities may be as individually and institutionally specific as the elements that foster the gap. Yet, an important first step is for college and university administrators to recognize the likelihood that a gap will exist, regardless of the nature of the vertical or horizontal move. By becoming aware of the factors that contribute to the dissonance experienced in the early socialization period of a new job, an administrator can learn to more successfully adapt to the new position. This process may begin early by recognizing the need to gather specific kinds of information during the job interview, and, once in the job, involves ongoing clarification of job responsibilities and requests for performance feedback. In general, the administrator must adequately prepare for and address the ambiguity and dissonance inherent to a new position. In addition, understanding the organization's cultures, wisely choosing confidants, establishing effective communication networks, and assessing and working with the professional anchoring of the position are strategies useful to all college and university administrators in bridging the gap between expectations and realities.

References

Amey, M. J. "Academic Vice Presidents in Action: An Analysis of Four Areas of Leadership Competency." Unpublished doctoral dissertation, Department of Higher Education, The Pennsylvania State University, 1989.

Austin, A. E., and Gamson, Z. F. *Academic Workplace: New Demands, Heightened Tensions.* ASHE-ERIC Higher Education Research Report No. 10. Washington, D.C.: Association for the Study of Higher Education, 1983.

Clark, B. "The Making of an Organizational Saga." In H. J. Leavitt and L. R. Pondy (eds.), *Readings in Managerial Psychology.* (2nd ed.) Chicago: University of Chicago Press, 1980.

Clark, S. M., and Corcoran, M. "Perspectives on the Professional Socialization of Women Faculty: A Case of Accumulative Disadvantage?" *Journal of Higher Education*, 1986, *57* (1), 20–43.

Kanter, R. M. *Men and Women of the Corporation*. New York: Basic Books, 1977.

Krinsky, I. W. "What Are Colleges Seeking in Their Leaders?" *Journal for Higher Education Management*, 1986, *1* (2), 23–26.

Kuh, G. D. "Guiding Assumptions About Student Affairs Organizations." In G. D. Kuh (ed.), *Understanding Student Affairs Organizations*. New Directions for Student Services, no. 23. San Francisco: Jossey-Bass, 1983.

Louis, M. "Surprise and Sense Making: What Newcomers Experience in Entering Unfamiliar Organizational Settings." *Administrative Science Quarterly*, 1980, *25*, 226–251.

Moore, K. M. "Careers in College and University Administration: How Are Women Affected?" In A. Tinsley, C. Secor, and S. Kaplan (eds.), *Women in Higher Education Administration*. New Directions for Higher Education, no. 45. San Francisco: Jossey-Bass, 1984.

Morrison, A. M., White, R. P., Van Velsor, E., and the Center for Creative Leadership. *Breaking the Glass Ceiling: Can Women Reach the Top of America's Largest Corporations?* Reading, Mass.: Addison-Wesley, 1987.

Rasch, C., Hutchison, J., and Tollefson, N. "Sources of Stress Among Administrators at Research Universities." *Review of Higher Education*, 1986, *9* (4), 419–434.

Scott, R. A. *Lords, Squires, and Yeomen: Collegiate Middle Managers and Their Organizations*. AAHE-ERIC Higher Education Research Report No. 7. Washington, D.C.: American Association for Higher Education, 1978.

Walterscheid, E. "Hazardous Duty: It's a Dean's Lot." *Kansas Alumni*, 1990, *88* (8), 1–4.

Marilyn J. Amey is assistant professor of higher education in the Department of Educational Policy and Administration at the University of Kansas, Lawrence.

The careers of women and minority administrators all too often depend on whether they can successfully negotiate various double-bind situations.

Creating Strengths Out of Our Differences: Women and Minority Administrators

Kathryn M. Moore

Until recently, most women and minorities who have served as administrators in colleges and universities have had relatively constricted work lives. By and large they have worked for one institution, or in one position, or in one type of institution. They seldom have held presidencies unless in a college serving their particular group. They have held few positions of national leadership or moved readily within such circles. Notable exceptions exist, of course. But in general the careers of women and minorities have been different from those of majority males. They have been more restricted, less diverse, and less influential in a national sense.

Today, however, circumstances are changing. Many more women and minorities are getting opportunities to make job changes, to consider several career alternatives, to weigh whether they wish to pursue top leadership positions; in short, they are pondering fully developed careers in higher education. Overall, these changes are occurring along essentially three dimensions: There are greater *numbers* of women and minority group members serving as administrators, and many more who will do so in the future. Their range of *opportunities* to create diverse careers is also expanding. And, most important, they are increasingly exercising significant *power and influence.*

Because women and minorities have been for so long outsiders to the central leadership roles of higher education, they have had to think hard and long about what it takes to be an administrator under those exclusionary circumstances and what it will take to change the social environment

New Directions for Higher Education, no. 72, Winter 1990 © Jossey-Bass Inc., Publishers

of higher education. There is wisdom to share, and not only for the benefit of other women and minorities. The purpose of this chapter is to examine the three types of changes both for what they mean now and for what they may portend. I intend to show how particular experiences and qualities of women and minority administrators today can be used by them to build stronger careers and better institutions in the future.

Numbers: Positive and Negative Signs

The number of administrators who are women or people of color has been increasing steadily since about 1972, when various federal and state agencies began to hold institutions accountable for hiring practices by means of affirmative action guidelines and other initiatives. Still, the number of women and minorities who occupy senior leadership positions is quite small. The American Council on Education reports an average of 1.1 women in senior positions per institution (Pearson, Shavlik, and Touchton, 1989). Over 300 institutions have women presidents and about 144 have black or other minority presidents (Green, 1988; Wilson and Melendez, 1988). In about fifteen cases this involves a double count of leaders who are both female and minority group members. In the middle ranks, the numbers of women and minorities are considerably better, encompassing approximately 30 percent of all positions (Wilson and Melendez, 1988). Indeed, the difference in diversity between the cohort of senior-level administrators on most campuses and administrators at the other levels is often quite pronounced. Given this growing diversity at the entry and middle levels of administration, some say it is only a matter of time before diversity is found at the executive level. But is this prediction valid?

A principal assumption of the pipeline argument is that the present low numbers are the result of a lack of candidates from which to choose. Once sufficient numbers of qualified candidates are in place in lower levels, then the upper levels will begin to change also as likely candidates move up. This is a useful argument in important respects, especially if it serves to silence those who have resisted change on the grounds that there are not any qualified women and minorities out there. But research by Fulton (1986) suggests that even when search committees do their job of identifying qualified candidates, identification is not productive unless the responsible administrators are willing to make the appointments. Many say that a glass ceiling does exist between the middle levels and top jobs (Morrison, White, and Van Velsor, 1987).

Another argument for optimism about a future increase in the number of women and minorities in top leadership positions is the expectation that there will be a large number of vacancies in these positions. Although impending faculty vacancies are receiving considerable media attention, it is also true that many administrators are the same age, if not older, than the cohort of faculty who will be retiring in the next few years. A large number of vacancies should make it easier and more likely that women and minorities will get new places in the senior ranks of administrators. But will it?

Other observers of the academic marketplace point out that turnover rates for administrators are already quite high. The average presidential term has been falling steadily and is now below seven years (Kerr and Gade, 1986). Other positions already have high replacement rates, but no major changes have occurred in the diversity of the occupants. In an examination of the social origins of administrators, Twombly and Moore (in press) noted that the enormous expansion of higher education in the post–World War II years did not result in significant diversity at that time. Moreover, Twombly and Moore's analysis of newly created administrative positions as of 1983 showed that although there have been impressive increases in new positions, white males tended to get them more often than either women or minorities.

In the short run, at least, it seems likely that the numbers of women and minority administrators who occupy upper-level positions will increase, but slowly. As a result, these individuals still will have to contend with the difficult dynamics of tokenism so graphically depicted by Kanter (1977) and others (for example, Sandler and Hall, 1986). These include heightened visibility combined, paradoxically, with greater personal isolation, and accentuated opportunities for influence combined with greater risk of making mistakes. For many women and minority administrators tokenism involves a difficult balancing act. They must maintain and grow in their positions while urging their institutions to continue to diversify, and they must do both while not appearing to be either self-serving or focused on only their "special interests." As Mary Catherine Bateson (1989, p. 205), a former dean at Amherst College, notes, "We live in a world in which many positions are open to women, but there is always the slight stacking of the deck, the extra stress, the waiting prejudice that amplifies every problem."

The careers of female and minority administrators all too often depend on whether they can successfully negotiate various double-bind situations (Jones and Welch, 1986; Sandler and Hall, 1986). As tokens in leadership groups, the one or two women or people of color are often made to figure out by themselves how to be effective advocates for their demographic groups and how to work effectively as equal members of leadership teams. The challenges are particularly delicate when related social issues arise on campus. Incidents of racism or sexism often create the temptation among the majority members of a leadership group to make the token responsible for "fixing" the problem, even as the disaffected campus group also expects the token to ensure that its demands are met.

Trivial day-to-day events also remind female and minority administrators that the responses of others are based on their race or sex, not on their abilities. Comments about appearance, thoughtless or malicious remarks about life-styles, and patronizing attempts to single out such individuals for particular praise or blame are likely indications that diversity is not yet a normal condition on most U.S. campuses (Moses, 1989; Morrison, White, and Van Velsor, 1987). Poise, a sense of humor, and the support of a few trusted and sympathetic friends are what many women and minorities say carries them through both the small and the large difficulties of their socially marked status as administrators (Sandler and Hall, 1986). They also find strength in the knowledge that a sure cure for the pathologies of tokenism is to add more women and more minorities until their numbers transform the unusual into the commonplace.

Opportunities: Making the Most of Difficult Situations

Rather than merely waiting for the numbers to increase, let us consider some steps that individual female and minority administrators can take to turn the negative aspects of their situations into positive ones. For example, the visibility that comes from being one of only a few female or minority administrators on campus is not always a bad thing. Personal opportunities can grow from being visible. For example, being visible can provide access to people and to agencies that less visible people do not have. Being known can open doors. It may make it easier to be heard as well as seen.

To be sure, this visibility involves added pressure to be articulate, prepared, and competent (Shavlik and Touchton, 1988). Serving on task forces, committees, and advisory groups as a token representative need not mean the person must remain so designated. By demonstrating the ability to address the wider issues of the work group, by being willing to work on other tasks, the female or minority administrator can earn respect and build working relationships with other important people. This is not very different from the way mentors open doors for their protégés or the means by which other people have gotten their breaks into better opportunities. The catch is for the administrator to avoid believing that all the attention means he or she is exceptional (Sandler and Hall, 1986). The trick is to use the visibility to pave the way for others.

Judicious use of the advantages of visibility includes addressing groups of people on and off the campus. Cultivation of the skills of public speaking is never wasted by any leadership aspirant. Such public speeches afford opportunities to teach about and to highlight important problems or solutions and to enlist cooperation from people one is not likely to encounter otherwise. By becoming articulate and effective spokespersons for their institutions, women and minorities also are mastering important leadership skills they will draw on throughout their careers.

Opportunities to lend personal support to others is another positive outcome of being visible and different. All successful causes must have advocates and supporters. Choosing wisely when to lend support to others is a necessary skill of effective administrative leaders. Many good causes die for lack of support, not for lack of merit. Often the issues of race and sex are cast as competing interests on campus. Advocacy of important ideas for blacks may seem to involve a lessening of support for women, or vice versa. It is easy to get caught up in struggles over a tiny slice of the pie, when others are deciding how the whole pie will be divided. Learning to keep their "eyes on the prize" is another valuable lesson for "different" administrators to acquire.

Visibility also can provide opportunities to build coalitions with other groups and individuals to solve common problems. Such coalitions can lead to even better solutions than anyone could have envisioned alone. For example, on one campus when both Hispanic and black women identified a common need for day-care services, their combined voices brought support by several predominantly white women's groups, which in turn led to the creation of a day-care center to serve all the community. Administrators use negotiation and coalition building throughout their careers so that, difficult as it is for people starting out, time spent on developing these skills is worthwhile. Bateson (1989, p. 231) points out that "the central survival skill is surely the capacity to pay attention and respond to changing circumstances, to learn and adapt, to fit into new environments."

Isolation is the paradoxical side of visibility. It is painful not to be or feel part of a group. But it is often equally difficult to try to appear to be a part of the group when one is not. Being the only woman in an all-male administrative group, or the only person of color, is seldom easy no matter how accepting the other people are. But isolation has its positive side also. Recall the experiences of Martin Luther King, Jr. Busy and productive, surrounded by crowds of people for much of his life, he made some of his greatest contributions, such as "Letter from a Birmingham Jail," when he was physically as well as spiritually isolated. The experience of separation can foster great strength and insight. By being an outsider, such a person "is relieved of the burden of constantly justifying loyalties she does not feel and cannot share. She becomes, in other words, her own woman" (Swoboda and Vanderbosch, 1986, p. 3).

Opportunities—the growth-producing ones at least—usually involve some degree of risk. Risk involves the possibility of error or loss. It is easy to tell someone "nothing ventured, nothing gained," but it is harder to actually do the venturing. Female and minority administrators, because of their heightened sense of vulnerability and visibility, often feel that they cannot afford to make any mistakes. They feel compelled to excel at whatever they undertake. Organizations, for their part, are quick to exploit such beliefs, draining the individuals' efforts while retaining the power to get rid of them when they are exhausted. It is only when the individual is able to develop a sure sense of identity that is not defined exclusively by the organization that he or she is able to confront risky opportunities with the proper spirit. Like the professional sky diver, it is possible for an administrator to accept that not all risks can be eliminated, but they can be assessed and even minimized, contingencies can be planned for and preparations made. It is then possible to abandon oneself to the task with a spirit of adventure as well as learning. The key is to avoid sudden stops!

To join with others is to begin to articulate a broader vision of caring that scholars such as Gilligan (1982) and leaders such as Johnnetta Cole (in Bateson, 1989) have argued is part of the cherished heritage of both women and minorities. Lifting up the vision of a caring campus may be the unique contribution that "different" administrators can contribute. From Virginia Woolf to Adrienne Rich to Alice Walker, numerous writers have spoken to the strengths that outsiders develop that ought not be cast aside once they become insiders. In addition to an ethic of care, a sense of community is also invaluable. Great tasks can be accomplished by a group that is united. Seemingly impossible difficulties can be surmounted if the burdens are shared. This sense of caring and community may provide the ethos that is needed to enable embattled institutions to face and overcome difficult fiscal or intellectual challenges. Such gifts are the heritage of those who have struggled outside the gates, and they offer significant consequences for women and minority leaders and for their institutions once such people are inside the gates and in substantive administrative positions.

Power: Handle with Care

All administrative positions have some power no matter what level or location. One has only to recall trying to register late for a class or park in an unauthorized place to appreciate that power flows like an electric current throughout our institutions. But as John Gardner (1990) has pointed out, most leaders have power, but not all the powerful are leaders. Learning the difference between power and leadership is doubtless a lifetime assignment in which practice in both is essential. Although lengthy discussion of either of these fascinating topics is beyond the scope of this chapter, let me raise a few of the issues that confront women and minority administrators as they come into their own as leaders and seek to use power wisely and well.

The first issue is apprenticeship or learning from others (see Johnsrud, this volume). People who want to wield power need to learn how to handle it, much as an electrician teaches an apprentice by working with live current. The apprentice needs to learn not to fear the current but rather to respect its power and what it can do if it is mishandled. Since power, electric or other, can be lethal, it is wise to watch a while before handling it directly and then, if possible, to handle low voltages before moving to stronger ones. Observing and learning from a veteran leader is one of the best ways to examine the connections between leadership and power.

Veteran majority male leaders may not always be able to teach aspiring female and minority administrators what the correct decisions would be under specified circumstances, but the veterans can share what kinds of decisions they have made, why they made them, and what happened before, during, and after. The astute apprentice is perhaps less interested in the what of a decision, but he or she can benefit from the why and the how for learning about people in situations. Although, as Johnsrud (this volume) points out, mentor relationships are not for everyone, everyone can use close observation and probing questions to elicit information from veteran administrators. "Tell me more" is one of the most flattering requests older administrators can receive.

Knowledge of academic organizations in action is another important aspect of leadership. Experience in context is so valued in higher education administration that it explains why administrators are frequently chosen because of their experience in a particular type of institution rather than for any given particulars of expertise. As many contributors to this volume have made clear, the nuances of the administrative marketplace are tied to the particularities of the various institutions. Administrative positions are profoundly shaped by the culture of institutions. Being a good analyst of organizational culture is, therefore, exceedingly helpful. Although women and minorities are frequently viewed as different and treated as outsiders, knowing how an organization reacts to difference, to change, and to challenge are indispensable pieces of intelligence for any administrator intent on not only surviving but also thriving.

Leaders who are demographically different from those to whom the members of the institution are accustomed must be able to shift the attention from superficial differences to the real subject matter of the leadership roles they seek to carry out. As Kauffman (this volume) shows, they can gain credibility and cooperation as they show their sensitivity to and support for the deepest values of the institution. But showing concern for the campus as a community does not mean blind acceptance of its norms and values. Challenge is as important as support from leaders who seek to promote the best in that community (see Sagaria and Johnsrud, 1988). Legitimizing latent or missing ideas and voices, rewarding others who work constructively toward change, and striving to establish acceptance of diversity as strengths for the campus are especially important contributions that female and minority leaders can make.

Derek Bok (1986), former president of Harvard University, has commented that when administrators are asked to describe the high points of their careers, invariably they cite their efforts at educational reform. Leaders are expected to use their power and influence to bring about improvements in the institutions for which they are responsible. Opinions will differ on what constitutes an improvement, but not on the responsibility to make the effort. Female and minority administrators can find in this responsibility the opportunity to offer, from the richness of their experiences, new ways of seeing and acting that will benefit academic communities: "Building and sustaining the settings in which individuals can grow and unfold, not 'kept in their place' but empowered to become all they can be, is not only the task of parents and teachers, but the basis of management and political leadership" (Bateson, 1989, p. 56).

Conclusion: Tightropes of Our Own Choosing

There can be deep pleasure in exercising our talents within a chosen institution, real satisfaction in seeing our skills and competence develop, honest pride in performing well (Tinsley, 1986). These sensations are no different for women or minority administrators than they are for majority males. But as we have seen, the opportunity to experience them has only recently become a possibility for very many women and people of color. Still, the few women and minorities who have had opportunities to exercise their talents in top leadership positions have found themselves forced to cope with difficult situations that are the result of their small numbers and token status rather than problems inherent to the challenges of administrative work. Columnist Ellen Goodman (1990) writes, "Whenever one of our number achieves a new status, others are convinced that at last and at least she is now immune from second-sexism. Then it turns out that she is just an outsider in an ever-more-inner sanctum. The treatment may be more subtle, more difficult to assess or to admit, but it is there."

The ultimate cure for this deep-seated problem of exclusion is a significant increase in the numbers of women and minorities who hold leadership positions, a real expansion in the kinds of opportunities available to such individuals, and a true sharing of power in the governance of our institutions. Until those conditions are met—indeed, on the way to meeting them—it is vitally important that women and minority administrators now in place find the means and the opportunities to surmount the dynamics of tokenism as best as they can. Essentially, this task involves accepting as a given of the present situation a set of paradoxes concerning visibility and isolation, opportunity and risk. But it also involves refusing to accept that the present conditions must and will persist. The central aim is to develop a critical distance from the circumstances of today while working toward a preferred future of greater diversity and deeper equality tomorrow.

"Tightropes of our own choosing" (Swoboda and Vanderbosch, 1986) is a phrase that captures for me the essence of what is required in higher education. People can and do adapt successfully to circumstances in the present while refusing to become assimilated to them. This adaptation requires a vision of the future toward which to strive. It requires moving along the tightrope of expectations and realities with only one's talents and values as a balancing rod. It means converting adversity to opportunity wherever possible. Those who are already in place, high or low, alone or in groups, can make use of their circumstances, including visibility and isolation, and opportunity and risk, to grow as individuals and to bring about through the activities of their own careers the kind of richly diverse future most of us desire. As we are slowly learning, the problem is not only to ensure the hiring of women and minorities, difficult as that task is, but also to turn our colleges into places where all those who are hired, men and women, minority and majority, can "go from strength to strength" (Bateson, 1989).

References

Bateson, M. C. *Composing a Life.* New York: Atlantic Monthly Press, 1989.
Bok, D. *Higher Learning.* Cambridge, Mass.: Harvard University Press, 1986.
Fulton, B. F. "Access for Minorities and Women to Administrative Leadership: Influence of the Search Committee." In P. Farrant (ed.), *Strategies and Attitudes: Women in Educational Administration.* Washington, D.C.: National Association for Women Deans, Administrators, and Counselors, 1986.
Gardner, J. W. *On Leadership.* New York: Free Press, 1990.
Gilligan, C. *In a Different Voice.* Cambridge, Mass.: Harvard University Press, 1982.
Goodman, E. "Powerful Female Voices Still Unheard." *Lansing State Journal,* Sept. 28, 1990, p. 2.
Green, M. F. *The American College President: A Contemporary Profile.* Washington, D.C.: Center for Leadership Development, American Council on Education, 1988.
Jones, J., and Welch, O. "The Black Professional Woman: Psychological Consequences of Social and Educational Inequities upon the Achievement of High-Status Careers in Leadership Positions." In P. Farrant (ed.), *Strategies and Attitudes: Women in Educational Administration.* Washington, D.C.: National Association for Women Deans, Administrators, and Counselors, 1986.
Kanter, R. M. *Men and Women of the Corporation.* New York: Basic Books, 1977.
Kerr, C., and Gade, M. L. *The Many Lives of Academic Presidents: Time, Place, and Character.* Washington, D.C.: Association of Governing Boards of Universities and Colleges, 1986.
Morrison, A. M., White, R. P., and Van Velsor, E. "The Narrow Band." *Issues and Observations* (Center for Creative Leadership), 1987, 7, 1-7.
Moses, Y. T. *Black Women in Academe: Issues and Strategies.* Washington, D.C.: Project on the Status and Education of Women, American Association of Colleges, 1989.
Pearson, C. S., Shavlik, D. L., and Touchton, J. G. (eds.). *Educating the Majority: Women Challenge Tradition in Higher Education.* New York: American Council on Education and Macmillan, 1989.
Sagaria, M.A.D., and Johnsrud, L. K. "Generative Leadership." In M.A.D. Sagaria (ed.), *Empowering Women: Leadership Development Strategies on Campus.* New Directions for Student Services, no. 44. San Francisco: Jossey-Bass, 1988.
Sandler, B. R., and Hall, R. M. *The Campus Climate Revisited: Chilly for Women Faculty, Administrators, and Graduate Students.* Washington, D.C.: Project on the Status of Women, American Association of Colleges, 1986.
Shavlik, D. L., and Touchton, J. G. "Women as Leaders." In M. F. Green (ed.), *Leaders for a New Era: Strategies for Higher Education.* New York: American Council on Education and Macmillan, 1988.
Swoboda, M. J., and Vanderbosch, J. "The Society of Outsiders: Women in Administration." In P. Farrant (ed.), *Strategies and Attitudes: Women in Educational Admin-*

istration. Washington, D.C.: National Association for Women Deans, Administrators, and Counselors, 1986.

Tinsley, A. "Upward Mobility for Women Administrators." In P. Farrant (ed.), *Strategies and Attitudes: Women in Educational Administration.* Washington, D.C.: National Association for Women Deans, Administrators, and Counselors, 1986.

Twombly, S. B., and Moore, K. M. "Social Origins of Administrators." *Review of Higher Education,* in press.

Wilson, R., and Melendez, S. E. "Strategies for Developing Minority Leadership." In M. Green (ed.), *Leaders for a New Era: Strategies for Higher Education.* New York: American Council on Education and Macmillan, 1988.

Kathryn M. Moore is professor of educational policy and leadership in the Department of Education Administration at Michigan State University, East Lansing.

It is imperative that those who seek academic administrative posts or advancement articulate their fidelity to the central purposes of their colleges and universities and to the values of scholars and learners.

Administration Then and Now

Joseph F. Kauffman

It is difficult to encapsulate the rich and interesting history of higher education administration in the limited space of a book chapter. Duryea (1973) has described the evolution of university organization in a valuable essay, and I have attempted to describe the college presidency as it was and as it is (Kauffman, 1982).

Most historians of higher education trace the first major administrative appointments made by presidents to the year 1878, when Harvard president Charles Eliot appointed Professor Ephriam Gurney as dean and Cornell president Charles White appointed Professor William Russell as vice-president. Colleges and universities were small entities compared to today, and the president was *the* administrator, often teaching as well. To grasp the difference in size with today's multiversities, I cite the University of Wisconsin, which in the academic year 1876–1877 had a total student enrollment of 316.

For a variety of reasons, including the nature of funding, administrative staff at American colleges and universities grew rapidly in the twentieth century. At first, faculty members were pressed into service as registrars, library directors, and the like. As enrollments grew, particularly after World War II, and faculty shortages became apparent, a whole new class of professional administrators developed. Today, professional administrative staff are a significant proportion of the professionals employed by colleges and universities, and they often deal with matters that were not a part of a college's responsibility in the previous century. Grassmuck (1990) indicates that their number had increased by 61.1 percent from 1975 to 1985, compared with an increase of 5.9 percent for faculty members.

Faculty Attitudes Toward Administration

Scholars have traditionally viewed administrators with suspicion, if not hostility. This is especially true in research universities and liberal arts colleges. The growth in the size of administrative staffs, with their accompanying bureaucratic procedures, exacerbated the natural antipathy of faculty toward administrative personnel. Jencks and Riesman (1968, pp. 17–18) aptly portrayed this antipathy: "Academicians are neither a tolerant nor an easy-going species, and their apparently congenital feelings of irritation and frustration require scapegoats. Administrators serve this purpose and they serve it best when their actions can be attributed to non-academic considerations. So they are usually regarded as the enemy."

Jencks and Riesman wrote about faculty power at a time when it was beginning to atrophy, at least to some extent. With the possible exception of major research universities where individual scientists had developed their own sources of funding, most institutions began to feel the effects of budget volatility, state agency and legislative mandates for greater accountability, and a real, if undefined, desanctification of faculty prestige as student disaffection received wide media and government attention. The anticipation of steady-state or declining enrollments, coupled with what was described as a Ph.D. "glut," added to this picture.

Nevertheless, I think it is important to recognize and deal with the traditional faculty skepticism toward those who seem to seek power over scholars. Harold Stoke (1959, p. 20), a former president, wrote, "Those who enjoy exercising power shouldn't have it and those who should exercise it are not likely to enjoy it." This view is still part of the myth and fabric of searches for presidents and senior academic administrators. Those who seek such posts too aggressively are viewed with suspicion. One is to be "called" to such responsibility. That is why vacancy notices and advertisements enable nominations as well as applications. In presidential searches the mating dance is even more intricate at times, with the advent of search consultants approaching prospects on a confidential basis.

While it may be necessary to convince a governing board, or system administration, that one is committed to effective management and efficient operations, that is not sufficient to win the support of the campus itself. It is imperative that those who seek academic administrative posts or advancement articulate that their fidelity is to the central purposes of their colleges and universities and to the values of scholars and learners. The effective functioning of these institutions toward such purposes is the primary goal of administrators.

Growth of Nonacademic Administration

All of the above speaks primarily to the presidency and the areas of academic administration. With the possible exception of the small, independent, or church-related college, most institutions today have separated the academic from the nonacademic administration. On the academic side, provosts and vice-presidents for academic affairs, academic deans, and presidents of most four-year institutions are expected to have at least some faculty experience. In our most prestigious liberal arts colleges and research universities, those called to such posts are often seen as colleagues temporarily assuming administrative responsibilities. Their status is enhanced by being seen as "amateurs," rather than as careerists, in administration. It is assumed that they are fully capable of resuming their scholarship pursuits at an appropriate time.

It is in the nonacademic areas that administration has grown increasingly professional. At first, faculty members took on the duties of advising and supervising student organizations as a part of their faculty responsibilities in an era of in loco parentis. (I can remember when student dances and social events required the attendance of faculty chaperons.) A faculty scholarship committee distributed such scarce funds as existed for student aid. Counseling was left to those psychology professors who were interested and willing. It did not take long for faculty members to insist that such duties were a detraction from their scholarly roles, and we saw the burgeoning of student services staff, especially after World War II. Today, most universities have full-time, professional staff in admissions, financial aid, counseling, residence hall and student life, student health, and other support services.

A similar development took place in the financial and administrative services area. I can remember when a clerk made entries into a ledger, in long-hand—with a fountain pen, not a ballpoint pen. The need for information systems, reports to state and federal agencies, comparative cost data, and the like changed all of that. The advent of the computer and automated data processing changed the green eyeshade image of the business office forever.

University relations, development, and media relations all required full-time professional staff. Their successful functioning could not be left to chance or to amateurs. Similarly, personnel operations, publications, student records and registration, budget planning, and more required the full attention of competent staff. Here, as with all of the above administrative areas, there is no attraction for the amateur; appropriate specialized study, credentials, and successful experience are the criteria for such posts. Each specialty has its professional association, journals, conferences, and in-service workshops. There are hardly any generalists in administration today, unless one includes the various assistant-to positions that are often entry level or rely on personal relationships with the person assisted.

The Changing Environment

It is in the increasingly turbulent environment in which colleges and universities function where the most marked changes have occurred. This includes the extraordinary growth in both enrollments and in the number of institutions. Total enrollment grew more than 400 percent from the early 1950s to the present. The total number of postsecondary institutions grew by more than 80 percent in the same time period. Enrollment in public institutions now represents approximately 80 percent of the total.

All of this expansion led to new concerns about financing and public policy toward access, choice, and quality. Inevitably, this produced demands for accountability, comparative data, assessment of results, and greater centralization at the state level. It also led to the creation of university systems in the public sector. Today, the fifteen largest public systems of higher education in the United States together exceed in enrollment all of private higher education (Kerr and Gade, 1989, p. 119).

There are many career opportunities today at the level of the university system or state higher education agency. Whether one is speaking of homogeneous systems such as the University of California or the California State University, or consolidated state systems such as Wisconsin, North Carolina, or the State University of New York, there are important posts to be filled. Similarly, state higher education agencies in Illinois, Ohio, Texas, and elsewhere have professional staffs who play key roles with both institutions and elected state officials. There are national meetings of state academic affairs officers, state finance officers, and others. University systems and state systems are here to stay, and those seeking administrative careers should consider such opportunities for service.

The emphasis on access to educational opportunity began in the late 1950s and accelerated in the 1960s with the passage of civil rights legislation and the death of Martin Luther King, Jr. When I began my administrative career in the early 1950s, there was no state or federal financial aid for students. Private institutions awarded some scholarships in which merit was a major factor, and there were some emergency loan funds for limited purposes. Beginning with the National Defense Education Act in 1958, and escalating with the Higher Education Act of 1965, we have seen the federal role in student financial aid grow to billions of dollars. Together with various state programs federal financial aid has become essential to higher education, and it all has to be administered and accounted for. What would we do without it?

All of these changes required the assignment of college and university personnel to meet new opportunities and new challenges: counselors for returning veterans, financial aid administrators, auditors, state relations staff, planners, affirmative action officers, and on and on. By the late 1970s there were new concerns about excess capacity, unnecessary duplication, inadequate controls, and the increasing politicization of governance.

Management Concepts

Although faculties benefited from the expansion of higher education, there was skepticism and hostility toward some of the changes that accompanied the growth. This was especially true of the numerous bureaucratic management practices and structures that were created. In a widely read study conducted by Rourke and Brooks (1964), it was revealed that there was a trend toward "scientific management" in colleges and universities, as evidenced by the emergence of offices of institutional research, the increasing reliance on quantitative data in policy analysis, and the use of computers in administration. Commenting on the new style of university administration, the authors concluded that "the trend in the direction of what has been called scientific management in public higher education has been accompanied by certain changes in the style of university administration. The fact that such detailed information is now collected or disseminated about the internal affairs of public institutions of higher learning means that state officials and the community at large are much more aware today than ever was true in the past of the way in which the educational dollar is being spent" (Rourke and Brooks, 1964, p. 177).

Such observations seem rather quaint to those accustomed to state audits, legislative budget analysis, or newspaper publication of all administrator and faculty salaries. Today, presidents and senior administrators are expected to be literate about basic management tools and techniques. Concerns about efficiency and effectiveness have increased, as have the tensions between the values of a learning community and business management techniques. While one may not want to use cost/benefit language with members of the English department, it would be wise to be able to speak such language with one's governing board or the budget analysts from the state legislature.

We have but to look at the various seminars and workshops offered to administrators by various associations to see the new realities and expectations. The current management seminars offered by the National Center for Higher Education Management Systems include such topics as strategic planning, resource allocation, planning and integrating the campus computing environment, developing a student-tracking data base, and similar topics. The 1990 institute sponsored by the Association for Institutional Research focused on the total quality-management concepts espoused by W. Edwards Deming and Joseph Juran (Walton, 1986). All of this costs money, too, not only for personnel but for the increasingly expensive technology involved. While everyone complains about the costs, the expectations, requirements, and compliance regulations continue to increase, especially at the state level.

Calls for Administrative Leadership

Today there are new challenges and opportunities in the administrative and leadership ranks of our colleges and universities. We are all familiar with the calls for a reexamination of curricula and an improvement of undergraduate education. Most institutions are reviewing general education requirements or their core curriculum and developing ways to conduct assessments of learning. Whether responding to the criticism of Alan Bloom

(1987), E. D. Hirsch (1987), or Lynn Cheney (1988), such issues go to the heart of educators' reasons for being. But there are new goals enunciated as well, and equally biting criticism. The new expectations speak not to the content of curricula but rather to campus climate, civility, behavior, and lack of diversity.

A recent study by the Carnegie Foundation for the Advancement of Teaching and the American Council on Education (1990) identified a number of campus life issues that show a deterioration of conditions that must be addressed. One matter, which attracts the most media attention, is increasing conflict along racial and ethnic lines. This often expresses itself in the self-separation of students from one another, but there is also evidence of active expressions of hostility, harassment, and conflict. Other issues of concern involve substance abuse, primarily of alcohol, although new federal legislation requires each institution to establish standards of conduct prohibiting the unlawful use and possession of drugs and alcohol by students or employees, along with other rules. Failure to implement an antidrug program results in a loss of federal financial aid. Campus crime is another concern, including theft and assault.

For all of these challenges, action is called for and, frequently, the addition of administrative personnel to respond to the new needs and expectations. Although there have been increases in student services staff on some campuses, we also hear calls for greater faculty involvement in restoring a sense of community and for greater racial and ethnic diversity of faculty and staff. Whether for greater efforts at recruiting minority students, improving retention, being more aware of gender issues, providing child-care services, or other expectations, there is a call to respond to social and demographic change. Administrative leadership is expected to be dynamic, open, aware, and caring about these issues. So if learning a job and then doing it without interference are one's objectives, then college and university administration is best avoided. But if opportunities for important services are sought, higher education administration is a primary source.

Openness and Judicial Review

It is curious that along with the calls for a greater sense of community and caring we have also seen a change in the style of discourse and communication. As the courts have increasingly granted judicial review of college and university actions, legal staff have multiplied greatly. Faculty and staff personnel matters, student conduct issues, compliance with regulations concerning the handicapped, and many other actions may all come before the purview of the courts or regulatory bodies. It is unusual for a public institution not to be involved in several legal conflicts at any given time.

Prior to 1960, it was unusual for the courts to be willing to intervene in university matters. Kaplin (1985, pp. 3-10) has described the evolution of the law relating to higher education, from its early assertion of self-regulation to the present situation of state and federal regulations and statutes. Courts once accepted the proposition that attendance was a privilege, including the language in many college catalogs warning that students could be dismissed without specific assignment of cause.

During my years as dean of student affairs at the University of Wisconsin, Madison, the campus had no legal staff. The Board of Regents had one lawyer on their staff, concerned primarily with bequests and real estate matters. With lawsuits in both state and federal courts, related to student disruptions of authorized university functions, private counsel was engaged. At this writing, there are six lawyers on the campus administrative staff and three lawyers in system administration. Further, the state attorney-general's staff handles almost all of the university's actual litigation. Student discipline, faculty and staff personnel grievances, the patenting and licensing of discoveries, liability issues, compliance with a host of federal regulations and legislation, all have increased both the amount of litigation and the need to preempt litigation by prudent defensive actions.

What results from this litigious environment is a form of written and, at times, oral communication within the campus that has been drafted by legal counsel. The language is protective and defensive—just examine the typical letter of appointment from a public institution, for example. This sensitivity to legal ramifications affects the way administrators speak and write. There is a guardedness that, while perhaps necessary, is an obstacle to candid and caring communication. In the latter years of my career as an administrator I used to write personal, handwritten notes to accompany official letters of appointment. I would apologize for the formal, legalistic nature of the appointment letters and assure the appointees that we were delighted with their coming, despite the many caveats in the official letter.

One must add to this legalistic maze the fact that most public institutions operate in states with laws and regulations requiring open meetings, open records, and—for many—open personnel searches. In some states, confidentiality is simply not permitted. While one can make a case for such openness, it does affect administrative style, and individuals must adapt to these changes in order to work effectively. They must be prepared to have everything they do on the record.

Administration in Perspective

My intent here has been to highlight the challenges as well as the opportunities for those entering administrative jobs at this time. While I have emphasized the increasing professionalism and specialization of many administrative functions, there is still a difference between this work and academic disciplines. Within an institution, particularly a large one, it is possible for the general competence, resourcefulness, and character of an individual administrator to be noticed and rewarded. In such cases, a person can move across areas to levels of increasing responsibility. Some vice-presidents of business affairs are not certified public accountants. Some provosts are out of professional schools such as law, business, and engineering. Some presidents have won respect from their work in development or university relations. The academic world, despite its traditions, is not frozen in place. It does recognize talent.

Finally, it is important to add a word about colleges and universities as organizations. They are different from other kinds of organizations and the differences are important. They are also different from one another.

The essential purposes of colleges and universities are to provide teachers, scholars, and students with the resources, libraries, laboratories, classrooms, and environments needed for learning to take place. These pursuits are diverse, often individualistic, and not very amenable to management or control. Administrative concerns are frequently not seen as central to the enterprise. As Plante (1988, p. 78) has noted, "Colleges and universities were not created for the purpose of administering them." While there may be respect for sound management practices, management is not seen as the essential purpose of the institution, nor is it the reason why students and faculty are there. Administrators must understand this perspective and not resent it, however it may affect them as individuals.

It is also true that some types of institutions have a more bureaucratic, top-down form of administration than other types, which may be more collegial in style. The latter types require administrators to spend time in consultation with advisory bodies, often persuading rather than directing others. Obviously, administrative procedures are also different when faculty and staff are unionized and under collective bargaining agreements. An individual's own work style and aspirations will shape his or her interest in one kind of work setting over another.

Remember, administration is a means, as is governance. But that does not lessen its importance. Colleges and universities need men and women to assume responsibility for their effective functioning. Scholars need effective spokespersons to obtain resources and facilities and to administer policies and laws. Students need caring and resourceful mentors, advisers, and facilitators to enable them to make full use of the opportunities than an institution provides. Those who serve in this way have my deepest respect. It is a noble vocation.

References

Bloom, A. *The Closing of the American Mind: How Higher Education Has Failed Democracy and Impoverished the Souls of Today's Students.* New York: Simon & Schuster, 1987.

Carnegie Foundation for the Advancement of Teaching and American Council on Education. *Campus Life: In Search of Community.* Princeton, N.J.: Princeton University Press, 1990.

Cheney, L. V. *American Memory: A Report on the Humanities in the Nation's Public Schools.* Washington, D.C.: Government Printing Office, 1988.

Duryea, E. D. "Evolution of University Organization." In J. A. Perkins (ed.), *The University as an Organization.* New York: McGraw-Hill, 1973.

Grassmuck, K. "Big Increases in Academic-Support Staffs Prompt Growing Concerns on Campuses." *Chronicle of Higher Education,* Mar. 28, 1990, pp. A1, A32.

Hirsch, E. D., Jr. *Cultural Literacy: What Every American Needs to Know.* Boston: Houghton Mifflin, 1987.

Jencks, C., and Riesman, D. *The American Revolution.* New York: Doubleday, 1968.

Kaplin, W. A. *The Law of Higher Education: A Comprehensive Guide to Legal Implications of Administrative Decision Making.* San Francisco: Jossey-Bass, 1985.

Kauffman, J. F. "The College Presidency—Yesterday and Today." *Change,* May-June 1982, pp. 12-19.

Kerr, C., and Gade, M. L. *The Guardians.* Washington, D.C.: Association of Governing Boards of Universities and Colleges, 1989.

Plante, P. "In Support of Faculty Leadership: An Administrator's Perspective." In M. F. Green (ed.), *Leaders for a New Era: Strategies for Higher Education.* New York: American Council on Education and Macmillan, 1988.

Rourke, F. E., and Brooks, G. E. "The Managerial Revolution in Higher Education." *Administrative Science Quarterly,* 1964, 9 (2), 154-181.

Stoke, H. W. *The American College President.* New York: Harper & Row, 1959.

Walton, M. *The Deming Management Method.* New York: Putnam, 1986.

Joseph F. Kauffman is professor emeritus of educational administration at the University of Wisconsin, Madison. He also served as executive vice-president of the University of Wisconsin System and as president of Rhode Island College, Providence.

In order to grasp fully the opportunity for growth and development in academic administration, it is important to put higher education within a much larger framework: the global information society.

Administrative Careers and the Marketplace: Toward the Year 2000

Kathryn M. Moore, Susan B. Twombly

Today the administrative function in colleges and universities is larger and more complex than ever before. As Kauffman (this volume) notes, recent studies point to large increases in the numbers of executives, managers, and other professionals, compared to faculty. In the largest institutions whole categories or layers of personnel have been added. The growth is partly in response to a large number of state and federal laws "ranging from rules on the disposal of hazardous waste to measures meant to assure equal access to higher education for all students" (Grassmuck, 1990, p. A32). Though some condemn this growth as evidence of administrative bloat, others argue that "the demands placed on administrators to perform new and more intricate tasks will increase steadily and the need for competent, committed individuals to perform these tasks will not diminish" (Moore, 1984, p. 15).

In fact, to grasp fully the opportunity for growth and development in academic administration, it is important to put higher education within a much larger framework: the global information society (Cleveland, 1985). The institutions and activities that comprise higher education in the United States should really be viewed as the core of a much larger information enterprise, one that nearly all forecasters predict is going to expand tremendously in the future. If higher education is viewed from this perspective, then it is clear that the demand for individuals who can administer important elements of that enterprise will also expand.

Futurists and forecasters such as Cetron (1989), Naisbitt and Aburdene (1990), and Cleveland (1985) all point to the centrality of information in the twenty-first century and to the growing demand for individuals who can work with information, including the ability to manage it and work with it. In higher education we commonly refer to the forms of information manipulation and generation in which we engage as teaching, research, and outreach, but they are all vital parts of the larger information society. When administrative tasks are seen in this larger framework, administrators have the opportunity to see themselves as contributing not only to higher education directly but also to the substantial transformations our society is undergoing.

Regrettably, many administrators do not see themselves and their careers in this larger context because they are so intensely focused on their work within one institution. As Sagaria and Dickens point out in Chapter Two, the majority of administrators will spend their entire careers within one institution. Both for their institutions and themselves this can create an overly internal orientation to the administrative function. People begin to think that the boundaries of their particular institution are the boundaries of their world, when in fact the horizons of the information society reach far beyond. Moreover, Sagaria and Dickens argue forcefully that to be successful even in a single-institution career, an administrator must have many of the characteristics of other successful executives and managers, namely, flexibility, a positive attitude toward lifelong learning, and an awareness of the larger enterprise in which they are engaged.

Careers, Marketplaces, and Maps

As the authors of the preceding chapters have shown, many elements combine to form the multiple career systems that operate in higher education administration. Institutions play a defining role. To a large extent, they structure the parameters, duration, content, and outcomes of their administrative positions. Even the smallest college has more than one career system. From a national perspective this adds up to a complex, convoluted marketplace with many institutionally idiosyncratic features. Yet, amidst the enormous variety of titles and organizational structures, there are patterns to be found. Affinities exist among institutions by type and among positions by job families. Geographical boundaries and educational requirements also affect the selection and movement of individuals inside the marketplace.

For the newcomer to administration, whether a veteran faculty member assuming a position as department chair or a recent graduate taking a job as an admissions recruiter, this complexity can be baffling. It is not easy to see how one's position fits within the structure of a particular institution, much less the larger career systems in higher education generally. The particularities of each institution loom large in most administrators' efforts to function effectively. Moreover, institutions have not devoted a lot of attention to their career systems. They have tended to develop them on an ad hoc basis as the result of internal as well as external forces, including changes in top leadership, additions or subtractions of units or functions, and the legal and social demands of the society at large.

One of the latent but still important functions of affirmative action policies and procedures in colleges and universities has been the imposition of more order and process to recruiting, hiring, and promoting people, including administrators. When job descriptions have to be developed and formal searches conducted, when promotions have to be based on explicit criteria and reasons given for turning people down, then the employment system of the institution as a whole begins to acquire a structure that was lacking in the past.

As we move into the next century, the beneficiaries of clearer work structures in colleges and universities will begin to have other important effects on their institutions, some of which Moore outlines in Chapter Nine. Among the most important will be a greater diversification of people and talents. The remarkable homogeneity of race, class, and gender that characterized higher education in the United States for most of this century will not exist in the next. As Kauffman shows in Chapter Ten, much was accomplished by the white, male, largely middle- and upper-class faculty and administrators who have directed our colleges and universities virtually from their foundings. Equally strong accomplishments can be expected from the more demographically diverse people who will succeed them.

Lifelong Learning for Administrators: An Agenda for the Future

There has not been a great deal of scholarship devoted to the subject of administrative careers. As Twombly notes in Chapter One, what has been done is skewed somewhat in the direction of a few positions, such as the presidency and deanship, and within the contexts of particular types of institutions, usually the liberal arts college and the university. Since relatively few administrators will become presidents and many work in other types of institutions, the information has had only limited applicability for large numbers of people. Information such as that provided by Twombly, Dingerson, and Lawrence and Marchese in this volume, which is based on a potent combination of research and practical experience, is valuable in part because it is so rare.

The lack of information creates numerous knowledge gaps for administrators, such as the gap Amey describes in Chapter Eight. Unless an administrator is promoted directly from one related job to another in the same institution, Amey points out that there is likely to be a gap between the person's expectations about the job and its realities. Lack of general information contributes to this gap, but so does lack of care and concern for administrator preparation and socialization within institutions. Doubtless this is why mentors and confidants are so important to so many individual administrators, as Johnsrud describes in Chapter Six. The inside information and the personal attention to administrative skills that such veteran administrators provide to their protégés and subordinates are among the few means available for people to learn about their work and their own performance.

Another powerful means, described by McDade in Chapter Five, is to design a personal learning agenda and through personal efforts gain additional knowledge, skill, and understanding about administration. Though institution-based efforts are few, there are a rather large number of institutes, seminars, and conferences offered by universities, professional associations, and other organizations. Administrators can take advantage of these offerings and their institutions will benefit also. All too often, however, when money is tight, institutions are quick to eliminate attendance at such events. This can mean that the institutions as well as the individuals are cut off from ideas and techniques that could be helpful. But it is difficult to change the view that administrator development is a personal responsibility rather than a necessary and vital operating expense for every institution.

Individual interest and responsibility for self-development is still the principal means by which improvements in administrative performance are brought about. That is, individuals interested in their own effectiveness and growth must design for themselves the means to achieve those improvements without much aid or support from their colleges or universities. This can include working with a mentor or confidant, taking seminars, reading books such as this one, or enrolling for formal degree work in one of the many degree programs in higher education, educational administration, or related fields. Individuals benefit directly by becoming more informed and often more marketable, and not only within the confines of higher education.

But a larger issue remains unattended. This is the development within higher education institutions of a greater concern for their administrative structures and for the professional development of their own administrative personnel. Perhaps as more administrators engage in their own professional development, they will come to value and insist on greater efforts by their institutions to support and encourage such efforts and to build more effective employment structures. But building such a system person-by-person, institution-by-institution is a long and arduous process that few of us will live to see come to fruition.

Other influences need to be brought to bear. Perhaps the growing external forces of legislation and emulation of other, more effectively organized institutions in the information arena will provide an impetus to give more attention and resources to the examination of administrative structures and the development of administrative talent within colleges and universities. Perhaps the efforts of such overarching professional organizations as the American Council on Education, with its leadership development programs, or the training programs of various professional associations for business officers, student affairs, and academic and research administrators will in their aggregation promote such improvements. Perhaps the external pressures of state and federal governments or of consumers in general, through incentives for better services or the threat of reduced support for poor services, will encourage institutions to engage in more thoroughgoing efforts to improve and sustain their administrative cohorts.

Whatever it takes for higher education institutions, separately or in combination, to support growth and development in administration, it is clear that the future of the information society will depend heavily on talented, effectively prepared administrators to carry out the vital operations of those information enterprises we call colleges and universities. It is hoped that books such as this one and others to come will help those who are interested in the work of administration to do their jobs better and to make their lives more fulfilling, productive, and challenging. In the long run the institutions they serve will be the beneficiaries.

References

Cetron, M. *The American Renaissance.* New York: St. Martin's Press, 1989.

Cleveland, H. *The Knowledge Executive.* New York: Dutton, 1985.

Grassmuck, K. "Big Increases in Academic-Support Staffs Prompt Growing Concerns on Campuses." *Chronicle of Higher Education,* Mar. 28, 1990, pp. A1, A32.

Moore, K. M. "Careers in College and University Administration: How Are Women Affected?" In A. Tinsley, C. Secor, S. Kaplan (eds.), *Women in Higher Education Administration.* New Directions for Higher Education, no. 45. San Francisco: Jossey-Bass, 1984.

Naisbitt, J., and Aburdene, P. *Megatrends 2000.* New York: Morrow, 1990.

Kathryn M. Moore is professor of educational policy and leadership in the Department of Educational Administration at Michigan State University, East Lansing.

Susan B. Twombly is assistant professor of higher education in the Department of Educational Policy and Administration at the University of Kansas, Lawrence.

INDEX

ORDERING INFORMATION

NEW DIRECTIONS FOR HIGHER EDUCATION is a series of paperback books that provides timely information and authoritative advice about major issues and administrative problems confronting every institution. Books in the series are published quarterly in Fall, Winter, Spring, and Summer and are available for purchase by subscription as well as by single copy.

SUBSCRIPTIONS for 1990 cost $48.00 for individuals (a savings of 20 percent over single-copy prices) and $64.00 for institutions, agencies, and libraries. Please do not send institutional checks for personal subscriptions. Standing orders are accepted.

SINGLE COPIES cost $14.95 when payment accompanies order. (California, New Jersey, New York, and Washington, D.C., residents please include appropriate sales tax.) Billed orders will be charged postage and handling.

DISCOUNTS FOR QUANTITY ORDERS are available. Please write to the address below for information.

ALL ORDERS must include either the name of an individual or an official purchase order number. Please submit your order as follows:
Subscriptions: specify series and year subscription is to begin
Single copies: include individual title code (such as HE1)

MAIL ALL ORDERS TO:
Jossey-Bass Inc., Publishers
350 Sansome Street
San Francisco, California 94104

FOR SALES OUTSIDE OF THE UNITED STATES CONTACT:
Maxwell Macmillan International Publishing Group
866 Third Avenue
New York, New York 10022

OTHER TITLES AVAILABLE IN THE
NEW DIRECTIONS FOR HIGHER EDUCATION SERIES
Martin Kramer, Editor-in-Chief

U.S. Postal Service

STATEMENT OF OWNERSHIP, MANAGEMENT AND CIRCULATION

Required by 39 U.S.C. 3685

1A. Title of Publication		1B. PUBLICATION NO.						2. Date of Filing
New Directions for Higher Education		9	9	0	–	8	8 0	9/18/90

3. Frequency of Issue	3A. No. of Issues Published Annually	3B. Annual Subscription Price
Quarterly	Four (4)	$45 individual $60 institutional

4. Complete Mailing Address of Known Office of Publication (Street, City, County, State and ZIP+4 Code) (Not printers)

350 Sansome Street, San Francisco, CA 94104-1310

5. Complete Mailing Address of the Headquarters of General Business Offices of the Publisher (Not printer)

(above address)

6. Full Names and Complete Mailing Address of Publisher, Editor, and Managing Editor (This item MUST NOT be blank)

Publisher (Name and Complete Mailing Address)

Jossey-Bass Inc., Publishers (above address)

Editor (Name and Complete Mailing Address)

Martin Kramer, 2807 Shasta Road, Berkeley, CA 94708

Managing Editor (Name and Complete Mailing Address)

Steven Piersanti, President, Jossey-Bass Inc., Publishers (above address)

7. Owner (If owned by a corporation, its name and address must be stated and also immediately thereunder the names and addresses of stockholders owning or holding 1 percent or more of total amount of stock. If not owned by a corporation, the names and addresses of the individual owners must be given. If owned by a partnership or other unincorporated firm, its name and address, as well as that of each individual must be given. If the publication is published by a nonprofit organization, its name and address must be stated.) (Item must be completed.)

Full Name	Complete Mailing Address
Maxwell Communications Corp., plc	Headington Hill Hall Oxford OX308W U.K.

8. Known Bondholders, Mortgagees, and Other Security Holders Owning or Holding 1 Percent or More of Total Amount of Bonds, Mortgages or Other Securities (If there are none, so state)

Full Name	Complete Mailing Address
same as above	same as above

9. For Completion by Nonprofit Organizations Authorized To Mail at Special Rates (DMM Section 423.12 only)
The purpose, function, and nonprofit status of this organization and the exempt status for Federal income tax purposes (Check one)

(1) ☐ Has Not Changed During Preceding 12 Months	(2) ☐ Has Changed During Preceding 12 Months	(If changed, publisher must submit explanation of change with this statement.)

10. Extent and Nature of Circulation *(See instructions on reverse side)*	Average No. Copies Each Issue During Preceding 12 Months	Actual No. Copies of Single Issue Published Nearest to Filing Date
A. Total No. Copies *(Net Press Run)*	2000	2031
B. Paid and/or Requested Circulation 1. Sales through dealers and carriers, street vendors and counter sales	382	1106
2. Mail Subscription *(Paid and/or requested)*	1114	831
C. Total Paid and/or Requested Circulation *(Sum of 10B1 and 10B2)*	1496	1937
D. Free Distribution by Mail, Carrier or Other Means Samples, Complimentary, and Other Free Copies	82	63
E. Total Distribution *(Sum of C and D)*	1578	2000
F. Copies Not Distributed 1. Office use, left over, unaccounted, spoiled after printing	422	31
2. Return from News Agents	0	0
G. TOTAL *(Sum of E, F1 and 2—should equal net press run shown in A)*	2000	2031

11. I certify that the statements made by me above are correct and complete	Signature and Title of Editor, Publisher, Business Manager, or Owner *Larry Ishii* Larry Ishii Vice-President

PS Form 3526, Feb. 1989 *(See instructions on reverse)*